MW01148795

MOMENTS

and

MEMORIES

Ruth L. Weiss Hohberg

© Copyright 2018 by Ruth L. Weiss Hohberg
© Cover photograph by Ruth L. Weiss Hohberg.
Book design, typeset, layout by Barbara Quin

No part of this book may be used or reproduced in any manner
whatsoever without written permission except in the case of
brief quotations within critical articles or reviews.

ISBN-10: 1979830274
ISBN-13: 978-1979830270

Publication creative and technical assistance
provided by *GSP-Assist*, a service of

Great Spirit Publishing

Springfield, Missouri
greatspiritpublishing@yahoo.com

All rights reserved.

Published in the United States of America

My thanks to the Writers' Connection, the first critique group I joined in Rancho Bernardo. I first found the courage to write my stories while a part of this dynamic group.

Wordsmiths, another local group, has been a help in offering points of view.

A big thank-you and a tight hug to my good friend and neighbor Jerry, who has ideas for stretching my "writing" mind and believes that, despite his being incredibly well-read, I have something worthwhile to tell and will say it well.

Ruth L. Weiss Hohberg
San Diego, California
March 2018

TABLE OF CONTENTS

Part I
MOMENTS

Part II
MEMORIES THAT STAND OUT

PART I

MOMENTS

INTRODUCTION

I share this selection of remembered experiences with the intent to amuse and, with any luck, to offer support in thorny life passages toward "the light at the end of the tunnel."

As unique as we are, we have startling similarities; we all need to be appreciated, to love and be loved, to help, and to care. At rare moments, we make a connection and understand one another deeply. Those times are memorable and amazing parts of our human experience.

With thanks to those who were instrumental in creating the memories of the experiences, and the Writers' Connection and Wordsmiths in Rancho Bernardo, California, who encouraged me to continue to tell the stories.

A BREATH OF FRESH AIR

On a Friday evening in July of the last year of the 1980s, I responded to a special invitation to services for singles over-40 at a synagogue in Tarrytown, New York, that I had read about in the newspaper.

As per my custom, I arrived a few minutes earlier than the stated time. No one was there; the place was closed and quiet. That feeling of Oops! Wrong time, wrong date, wrong place surfaced. I consulted the calendar book I always carried in my bag. Everything seemed correct. I checked my watch; it was still a little early; I thought I'd stay a few minutes and see what happens.

A short, non-descript elderly man wearing a plaid sport jacket arrived. He looked around, his demeanor showing the same uncertainty I was feeling. He asked whether I was there for a Friday night service.

"Yes," I said, "do you think anyone will show up?"

In our mutual awkwardness to be the only two people in the synagogue lobby, we waited in silence. In a little while people began strolling in. He asked if he might sit next to me during the service. Again, I said, "Yes."

When the service ended, the congregants began to scatter; a few stayed for the traditional Oneg Shabbat, a customary post-service social time with refreshments. The man asked if I would consider joining him for a coffee at a nearby Howard Johnson's. At that time, HoJo was a nationwide chain of motels, hotels, and restaurants with a distinctive orange and turquoise color scheme that could be recognized on highways from afar.

Over coffee, he said he is widowed, lives in Florida, and has come to visit one of his four daughters in New York before embarking on a tour of Eastern Europe. He spoke about his late wife in positive terms, emphasizing her angelic qualities; but seemed adjusted to his single-person lifestyle and doing well. Among her good qualities, he mentioned that she never raised her voice or said anything unflattering about anyone; that she always expressed herself in ladylike language, never used strong words.

He told of how the single women in his community in Florida are aggressive to widowed or likely soon-to-be-widowed men, practically standing in line to offer casserole dinners. I had never heard such a thing. It sounded sad and comical as I pictured it in my mind's eye.

He asked about the circumstances of my current life. Maybe it was a reaction to hearing about the late lady's genteel way of expressing herself that I found myself in an unusual linguistic mood using uncharacteristic vocabulary when responding to his questions. I peppered my story with expletives like 'damn', 'hell', and whatever else I could think of in the category of unladylike words.

Later, at parting, I wished him a wonderful trip and, as a polite end to the evening, we exchanged phone numbers. When I drove away I asked myself, "Why did I do that? What inspired me to be outrageous?" I assumed that it was a rude linguistic shock to the poor man and made a very unfavorable impression. I then dismissed the encounter from my thoughts.

Weeks went by. One evening, he called to say he was back from a wonderful experience abroad. He told of where he went and what he saw describing his impressions in sensitive and varied vocabulary; his observational powers were obviously quite keen, and I was much more impressed with him than I had been in person the evening at the Howard Johnson's.

"When can I see you?" he asked.

"Are you serious? I thought my use of language had to have been offensive to you, considering the politeness you were used to with your wife. I didn't think you'd ever want to see me again."

"Oh no!" he said. "On the contrary, you were a breath of fresh air."

A DIFFICULT TIME - GETTING OUT

One Saturday afternoon at the end of May 1996, my 86-year-old, active, and interested-in-everything mother called to say that she was in great pain, could barely move; she didn't know what to do. Robert and I drove the 25 miles to her apartment in New York City right away. Mother couldn't straighten up and Robert carried her tiny frame to the car, so we could bring her back to our out-of-town home, feeling sure that whatever was the matter, she would recover with loving company, good food, and the fresh air of the suburbs. She had stayed with us several times before on occasions when she had fractured various parts of her anatomy.

Installed in an upstairs bedroom with a western view overlooking the grass and spring-flower-filled back yard, Mother had air and light. I tried to anticipate her every need and possible wish. Her determined refusal of medication, or to seek medical advice made it more difficult to help her. I let her rest the first few days in hopes that she would see reason and agree to try an over-the-counter pain medication and/or allow me to make an appointment to visit a health professional. She insisted on waiting without action.

A week later, at wit's end watching her suffer, I said, "I am going to call a doctor. At least we'll find out what the problem is; maybe he'll prescribe something to help you."

"No, no, I'll feel better tomorrow," was the response I had been listening to ever since she came. Not wanting to cause my mother any aggravation beyond her physical pain, I let it go and watched developments.

Three weeks later my emotional rope was stretched to its breaking point. "I don't have a clue what to do to help you. I am making an appointment with a doctor and you'll just have to come."

Faced with this near-ultimatum, Mother accepted a dose of Tylenol. It didn't help. The acute pains persisted; she agreed to see a doctor.

*****

"How are you today?" The ever-cheerful nurse at the geriatrician's office asked.

"Fine," was the barely audible response, a standard phrase my mother had adopted. Her absolute determination to play the Spartan was upsetting.

"No one goes to a doctor feeling fine," I mumbled to the nurse.

Several specialists and a difficult x-ray later, we had a diagnosis: compression fractures of the spine, a very painful condition, compounded by osteoporosis, malnutrition, and dehydration; a handful of issues to deal with simultaneously.

To whet Mother's appetite and increase her intake, I put frequent, attractive tiny snacks, along with drinks sometimes enriched with ice cream, on the table at mealtimes and in-between to tempt her. She wouldn't eat, she wouldn't drink. The snacks were left untouched despite my and Robert's encouragement. Although unusually compliant, in fact, impassive and apathetic in all other matters, she was actively resistant to nourishment.

Mother was so undemanding and self-effacing that it made Robert and me uncomfortable because we were convinced we could, and above all *wanted* to help her.

This was no longer the energetic talented woman who was positive and strong in the face of adversity, always engaged with the world, who, to make sure no time was wasted, kept me supplied with chores all day long when I was young.

To combat her depression, Mother willingly went to see a psychiatrist. He prescribed a few drops of Paxil, an anti-depressant medication, but the result was a total refusal of food and drink and the condition didn't improve. My commitment to respect my mother's self-determination as long as possible that I had learned in Social Work school was wearing thin. I was beginning to question her ability to make valid judgments.

In a support group, I discovered that Robert and I had the *ideal* patient. Other caregivers' parents were acting out in nasty ways, firing the household help at will on a daily basis, making middle-of the-night calls with outrageous claims, accusing their adult children of thievery, battery, and worse. We had tried all means we could think of to coax her to take nourishment or lift her despairing mood.

My mother was mostly silent, undemanding and, even worse, self-effacing. She didn't protest doctor visits and suffered unpleasant testing without complaint. The pain of the compression fractures became secondary to my concern with the malnutrition, dehydration, and the withdrawal of deep depression.

Perhaps her spirit would be re-inspired with her paints and like-minded company, I thought, and suggested attending a painting class for seniors. Mother agreed. When I took her there, she was warmly welcomed in the group, and for a moment it looked as if this might give her a lift. Returning two hours later, I saw her smearing the colors around aimlessly, without organization or interest. It was a devastating blow to witness how unfocused and indifferent she was. What was happening? It was so sudden. I was desperately trying to hold on to my beloved mother and best friend for as long as I could, not realizing that the woman I had known *forever* was no longer within my emotional reach. Something in her brain had deteriorated beyond the point of retrieval.

Her weekend sojourn at our home stretched into weeks and then months. The life Robert and I had envisioned when we married seven years before, to enjoy togetherness in our later years, was disappearing. The focus was completely on Mother. During the days, attention was on efforts to make her eat something, to bring a smile to her lips, or a glimmer of interest into her eyes. During the night, I listened for her footsteps on her way to the bathroom, worried about a possible misstep, a slip, or a tumble down the stairs.

I took Mother for an evaluation to a highly recommended, exceptionally gifted geriatric psychiatrist. His diagnosis was "the second stage of dementia." He explained that it was a progressive condition, with no chance of recovery or remission. He encouraged me to give myself "permission to grow up," as he put it.

The only child of Armenian immigrants, the doctor shared that, "No matter how much we do for our parents, it will never be enough. You need to do the best you can for your mother, but go and do what you need for yourself, live you own life."

The light went on in my brain. I understood. From that moment on,

I took charge of Mother's life, so I could begin to own mine. I realized how inadequate I was to the task ahead both physically and emotionally and that I couldn't do it alone.

"Senior Day Care" was a program designed for stimulation and structure. It sounded rational and helpful. When I proposed it, described it, and registered Mother to start the following week, she didn't voice any objections. The bus was there at eight in the morning. For the first time in her life, I saw Mother in an act in passive resistance. She dawdled while dressing and over breakfast. At 2:30 p.m., the bus brought her back. She objected to the "childish" games played there and reported having her hair pulled by one of the patients en route home. "I don't belong there," was a daily refrain. I went to see the program in operation. The former doctors, scientists, and academicians now patrons at the Day Care Center were deep into total disassociation from reality. It broke my heart to see this and Mother was not thriving. I took her out of the program.

What now? I asked myself. What can I possibly do to make things better for her and by extension for Robert and me? Mother's continuing unhappiness and apathy had a distressing effect on our home life. Robert and I considered it our sacred mission to make her feel happier.

I reviewed my life priorities so far, and found *must, should, ought to, need to,* and *must* have been the modus operandi as far back as I could remember. *Want to* or *feel like* was not part of the vocabulary. At 65, I wondered if I would ever have a turn to enjoy life with my husband before it was too late. In the past, I sought the wisdom of parental approval for decisions but now, I was the de facto parent. I had to face it: "I give myself permission to grow up NOW."

I began a search for an assisted living and skilled nursing facility nearby, always sharing my thinking and planning with my mother, in the hope for some response. Finally, after a few weeks, Mother stated her condition for making a change:

"If I am to move, it has to be to a private room."

Easier said than done. By now, my nerves were frazzled, and Mother's physical and mental condition was deteriorating quickly. Transporting her up and down stairs and into and out of the bathtub was a problem, even with Robert's help. I could no longer take care of her basic activities of daily living. At night, I worried to make sure she returned safely from the toilet. During the day, I worried that she might fall or burn through the teakettle again if left on her own alone even for a short time.

A facility with a distinguished history as a hotel for seniors since the early 20th century was four miles away. I visited. The social worker said that the timing was perfect.

"Bring Mother in for an interview."

At the interview, the formalities and banter went very well. The brightly smiling social worker asked in the professional voice that radiated that special *canned* enthusiasm, "How would you like to live here?"

Without a moment's hesitation, Mother said, "ABSOLUTELY NOT!" in a suddenly firm voice. My stomach convulsed into knots; I felt cornered yet saw no other option. She offered Mother a private room the following month. In a walk-through, the social worker showed us a light, pleasant room overlooking a fountain. I made the arrangements to move her to the home.

The comfortably furnished library was well stocked. Visiting hours were unlimited, a plus. I thought that Mother, an avid reader, would take pleasure in indulging her love of books.

The calendar of activities showed interesting discussions, exercise, and movie programs. I felt sure that with time, Mother, a charming lady, would find her niche and regain a measure of contentment as she had always managed to do in the past. There was a month to wait.

At home, we didn't have any further conversation about the projected move. I didn't want to increase her anxiety, but I worried. What if Mother refuses to go at the last minute, as a friend's mother had done? I was a nervous wreck during the weeks leading up to "M Day." This was a painful decision made with great reluctance, but something had to be done.

The move went smoothly. I spent several hours each day at the home, thinking that I was helping Mother adjust and find her way around. The residents were delighted to meet her. She smiled politely but didn't engage in conversation. After a week, she took a firm position. "I don't belong here. I must find a way to get out. These people argue, they yell at each other. These are not my kind of people."

"Where do you think you might be more satisfied?" I asked.

Mother shrugged her shoulders. It became her mantra at every visit. Her position was unequivocal. Robert and I were fully compassionate but saw no other options. I searched my soul to exhaustion thinking in ever smaller circles to devise a more satisfying alternative.

At home, Bob and I began to slowly reclaim our life, knowing that Mother was safe, clean, that food was presented to her, and we were always on call. She was miserable. She was also unhappy when living with us. What to do?

Six months later, a call during the night alerted us that Mother was on her way to the Emergency Room, because of having sustained the latest in a series of falls that had begun in 1988. I thought that by now she knew it was unsafe to go anywhere without the walker, especially at night.

"Did you use your walker?" I asked rhetorically the next day.

"No, I only went to the bathroom, not far." It was after the fact; the pleas of the past two years were for naught. Mother fractured her hip, a debilitating injury with a long recuperation period. She was moved to the skilled nursing level of care, the very thing Robert and I tried so hard to avoid, or at least postpone. With this fall, Mother's mental functioning took a steep dive. She lost any vestige of interest in anything; she would not even watch TV or speak when we visited. When her injury healed, I wheeled her outdoors for a change of scenery on sunny days. Mother's demeanor reflected unrelieved misery, conversational responses were not to the point and barely audible. The only clear message was: "I have to find a way to get out." It broke our hearts; we were impotent. With all our love and good intentions, Robert and I were powerless to halt the decline and lift her spirits which had been so positive in earlier times.

In October of 2002, Mother found her way *to get out*. She died.

A "ME" PIECE - A Ramble on Relationship

Early in our lives, we are told, "don't judge a book by its cover." That's very well meant, but the "cover" is the first thing that meets our senses. How can we help it?

In relationship between a male and a female, the first thought that comes to mind is sex. That's obvious and natural. In youth, and far into middle age, the prospect of a heterosexual relationship is inspired by visual/sensual/sexual stimuli as the primary source of attraction between a man and a woman. What is it that makes for the magnetism?

The first piece of information we receive about another is usually through the eyes. The girl and boy must have some visual feature that appeals to the other and draws them to approach. It's unique and indefinable; "chemistry," we say.

After the initial impression or stimulus by means of the visual Gestalt - the overall appearance – then can we hear the person's voice - even if only a "how do you do," observe body language, how they gesture, and what they're wearing. If those aspects appeal, we want to find out more: eventually we inquire and learn about their level of intelligence, world outlook, family background, and many other details. I'm not excluding exceptions, where a voice might provide that first "aha" or "oh no!" moment of fascination or its opposite by sound.

In my youth, the main appeal a boy had for me was in his eyes, often the blue-grey ones that seemed to have an inner light. The shape of the hands, how the nails were formed and groomed, and how he used his hands in gestures were some of the factors that entered my personal equation of who I found interesting. Decades later, in my dotage, I am still aware of these factors.

The intangible qualities that lead to a relationship surface later. Areas of interest, whether I can and am willing to participate in his, or learn new skills to accommodate them, plays a role. An important factor is appreciation and acceptance of the "other." It's considerateness. Those are qualities that reveal themselves if the initial impetus to enter a relationship is there.

Now the physical attributes are no longer as clearly visible, obscured and, in some cases, obliterated by wrinkles, eyeglasses, poor posture, and loss of a well-defined, youthful figure. There are instances when a person didn't make a visually favorable first impression yet turns out in time to be just "the one." It's a delightful surprise when I discover that the cover didn't tell very much of the story, and there's ever so much in that individual that I can like and/or admire.

When I was young, the message I learned regarding appropriate and acceptable behavior was from movies and reading. Relationship between boy and girl was well defined. It was a clear-cut scenario like this: the boy lusts after the girl, the boy kisses the girl, she slaps him and runs off…or she casts her eyes down, feels ashamed, and tells him not to ever do it again. She has to say it or be deemed "not a nice girl." He tries again, and… Who knows…?

I learned that I must "resist" any attempt of a boy to be physically affectionate because my reputation as a "nice" girl is at stake, easily lost, never to be regained. No one ever taught me what to do with my feelings of wanting to be in physical contact. Movies taught me that the girl "lets" or allows the boy to kiss her, generally as a big favor to him. He's the *kisser*, she the *kissee*. Participating actively was not part of condoned imagery. I wasn't aware that the desires a girl experienced were as natural a part of her growing into adulthood as the boy's.

Things have changed. Too many years later, I discovered that it's okay to return a kiss, initiate one, and even give a heartfelt hug without compromising my reputation as a "nice" old lady.

It took way too long before I rid myself of these taboos and gobbledygook and developed the ability to relate to the opposite sex person-to-person in an affectionate way without the primacy of the sensual/sexual aspect as the major part of the transaction. Fear of the loss of the relationship, were I to displease my "other," is also much lessened now that I'm old. I know that "what will be, will be."

My late-life relationships have a more multidimensional character, although the touching of minds is more likely to happen than the touching of bodies. Yet, there's a strong sense of intimacy that may not always have been present in the earlier relationships. How very nice! I almost missed that boat.

ELISE AND I AND LUNCH

"Help yourself! You must be starving!"

"I'm fine, don't worry. I had dinner last night," Elise answers in a tone that says, "Don't say that again."

I am having a historic lunch with my aunt and her two daughters. My cousin Elise is beyond slender, she's a skeletally thin woman – the kind that can be called a clotheshorse of senior vintage – clad neck-to-shoes in close-fitting black. Her stylishly-colored dark hair is clipped to half-inch length with a lick of bleached white close to the hairline. She picks up half a mini-bagel from the tray on the table, turns it around a few times, examines it, and places it with care, as if it were large and heavy, on her plate. She cuts it in half slowly, checks it appraisingly as if evaluating its significance, and makes what appears to be the important decision to top it with a tiny touch of cream cheese. It looks like a strange performance for as small an action as eating a mini-bagel for lunch.

"Come on, Alinko, eat something. It's almost one in the afternoon! You're wasting away. After all, you don't have to model the suits; you hire people to do that," her mother remonstrates.

My two cousins, Elise, her younger sister, and I are having this landmark get-together at the sunlit, art-filled condominium of my frail, nonagenarian Aunt T in a suburb of New York City. It has been many years since we have seen one another, and we are aware that it's most likely our last time. This is a bittersweet, rare moment occasioned by my visit to the East Coast.

Here we are, fossils meeting after many years, not quite sure what to say, to spend these moments of collective nostalgia most memorably. It's difficult to explain that the drama of the occasion seems to be more in my head than in its three-dimensional reality. I don't feel the emotional connection I thought I would or should. On reflection as to why, I think that it has to do with a lack of contact between us for so long; with no shared experiences to recall, and no exchanged words to keep connected, it's hard to care more than superficially. Unfortunately, our shared past-experience doesn't evoke particularly warm feelings in my memory.

"Did you say you have some family pictures to show me?" I ask my aunt, to provide a core around which our visit might take shape and perhaps provide some of the sentiment I hope to feel.

"Oh yes, I have a whole album." She reaches for her cane behind the chair, hoists her slender body onto her feet, and goes to fetch an old photo album. I am filled with anticipation, thinking there are pictures relating to my father's family to help fill some gaps in my history. Searching the pages for a face that might seem familiar, I am sorely disappointed. The pictures are only of her friends; none I may have known. I return the book.

Half of the half-bagel is still on Elise's plate, but she is "full" and must leave to drive back to the City to attend to business in one of her seven women's clothing stores on Madison Avenue. We bid each other farewell.

*****

As I settle into a chair, my mind wanders back through the years to my experiences with Elise and her mother that ultimately separated us, and the realization that what we now share is only a name. We are the remaining vestiges of a family that has run its course. The incentive that brought us to the table on that gloriously perfect, sunny, warm fall day may have been that we knew it's late and wanted to try to revive family feeling.

Sadly, the common bond simply isn't there anymore.

AN EVENING OF MAGIC

It's a festive evening. The moonlit sky and twinkling stars, a few passing wispy clouds reflect the light from earth, making interesting shapes in the clear firmament; stunning.

In the theater lobby, lights from the sparkling chandeliers reflect the colors of the jewels worn by the women to the ceiling as they move, like a dance. There's a palpable sense of excitement and anticipation in the lilting laughter of the ladies in contrast with the deep masculine guffaws of the men.

The colorful scarves adorning basic black outfits and vivid prints of dresses are a reminder that spring is here.

Hostesses circulate through the crowd, passing around trays with tiny plastic cups filled with samples of red and white Argentinean wine adding to the glow of the festive gathering. The walls of the lobby are filled with watercolors, photographs, and oil paintings of scenes of the surrounding community. The collective mood is far away from thoughts of strife, exploding bombs, hunger, captivity, and violent death that surround us in the real world.

The house lights dim. The curtain rises on an unlit stage; shafts of vertical light piercing its darkness create a mysterious space that magnetizes my gaze.

Ten dancers and five musicians take over. The magic is centered in the spotlights. Piano, bass, accordion, violin, and guitar provide the rhythm, a unique mixture of sensuous sound totally riveting my senses.

My eyes follow the dancers' slow, long steps punctuated by lightning-fast ones. The muscles of my body tense in what seems to be an involuntary attempt to mimic the action, eager not to miss a beat. The changes of direction, the tiny steps, rapid footwork, sudden ankle turns, and high leg kicks hold me in thrall. I can't keep up. They're much too fast. I am totally carried away by the spirit of the dance; my body, comfortably ensconced in the plush theater seat, feels every complicated move. It's as if I were dancing too. One number follows another with unabated energy; hardly a moment to catch my breath.

By intermission, I am exhausted, exhilarated, and thrilled to be witnessing this marvelous, magic art form. When the lights go on, I slowly become aware of being in a seat, and my muscles relax. I had forgotten about the audience around me. Was their experience like mine, I wonder as the movements and the music echo in my mind's eye and ear. It was a magical moment.

AN IMPORTANT DAY: May 8

From the cosmic point of view, there may be little or no perceptible difference between one 24-hour period and the next. From the human perspective, some days have far more significance in our personal and occasionally community lives than others. Some are even boundary points for a whole generation.

May 8, 1945, was such a day for me.

As part of Joseph Stalin's moving of populations, my family and I had been deported from our home in Europe in 1939, at the beginning of the war, transported to Siberia, and 18 months later to Uzbekistan in Soviet Central Asia.

On this day, I was ten-years-and-nearly-two-months old. My parents and I were living on an Uzbek collective farm in a primitive village that had a petroleum refinery and a railroad depot. I don't know if the place rated a dot on the map.

The day was sunny. It started with the usual awakening sounds of birdsong, the rooster, donkeys, sheep, and cows. An occasional neigh of a horse and working men's voices blended in with the sounds of early morning. The haughty camels looked down from their height and chewed, as always.

I was outdoors on this lovely spring day. I thought I heard someone in the yard say, "THE WAR IS OVER." Suddenly, everyone was running out of their doors shouting that it was so.

I had been waiting for this day in a state of almost suspended animation since I was four and a half. Yet, as the day unfolded, it was just too much "as usual" to contain such a momentous event. Was it true? I could not and didn't fully believe that on a common spring day the world had suddenly entered the long-awaited condition called PEACE. Had the killing really stopped?

As the morning hours slipped into afternoon and on into evening, and night came on as usual, I was overcome with disappointment, a letdown. How could it be that such a significant event occurred, and Nature didn't stop in her tracks? How could it be that the diurnal cycle wasn't interrupted to celebrate and make the day stand out from all others? In my childlike intensity of wishing and hoping the war would end, I thought and fully expected that it would manifest in some unforgettably dramatic way.

Nature didn't know about it. The birds and the flowers and the animals in the yard, as well as the people, continued about their affairs. This was just like any other lovely day in May.

Only when I got older did the impact become realized, and the day properly marked.

A NOT-SO-CHEERFUL TALE

Rebecca couldn't fall asleep after a particularly bruising evening of absorbing verbal abuse from her husband Zach. Her thoughts insisted on reviewing past events, digging into them to discern where in her marriage she went wrong. She asked herself when and how, instead of a loving and cooperative partnership she had intended to have at the start, it veered in another direction, to disintegrate to a permanent state of war punctuated by a series of intermittent moments of truce.

She fantasized that if she found where she had made her mistakes, they could, by having an honest no-fault-assigning conversation, reset their priorities and rescue their dream. No such thing was likely to happen, but her mind felt driven to review last evening's bombshell event moment by moment, hoping for an insight to start to make things better between them. This was late-night wishful thinking in the realm of imagination.

In the evening, while they were in the bedroom packing before their long-scheduled, all-expenses-paid trip to Bermuda, Zach had thrown a sudden, bizarre, and irrational tantrum. He slammed the suitcase shut, and shouted, "I don't like this. I'm not going with you. Go with your lover, your son,"

The words came out hateful, each word with the thrust of a stab; beyond shocking. Above all, the notion of such a thing was insane. Rebecca's temples throbbed, her body tensed, a dull pressure encircling her torso, as if she had been punched; nausea settled in her throat. She was at a loss as to what to think or do that would express her feelings and disbelief that such an awful, baseless accusation could be leveled at her. Her first impulse was to try to believe that she was imagining this disgusting scene, but, no, it was real.

She had to put some distance between herself and the source of this wicked, virulent invective, to be alone, and to physically lean on a sturdy, supportive wall. Muttering, "You're a sick puppy," she left the room and walked slowly and deliberately down the stairs to the kitchen, to catch her breath, to begin to try to sort out and to deal with this sudden unprovoked nightmare while awake.

In her despair, she thought, What about tomorrow? Would there be another scene? The taxi was ordered last week and would be waiting. What would he do in the morning? Would he be there? Should she go ahead with the trip if he doesn't come? Should she call it off? What if she had to go it alone?

Finally, shortly before dawn, exhausted with her frantic thoughts she decided, "Que sera sera…what will be will be," as the song goes, and fell asleep. For her, last night's experience was catastrophic.

The projected trip was a prize she had won in a drawing sponsored by the local Chamber of Commerce several months before. It was to be Rebecca and Zach's first time alone together with no household or child-oriented chores and duties since their marriage 17 years before. Bermuda sounded like heaven on earth.

In the morning, she saw Zach dressing; he said nothing. It appeared that perhaps he had changed his mind about not going. She decided to do what they called "trust the process" in social work school. She stayed silent and prepared for departure.

Rebecca couldn't explain the wide and deep emotional and physical chasm Zach had shaped between himself and her in the last few years. The romantic location of Bermuda was her hope of a week of healing, away from the home that had become a zone of conflict. There, he found everything unattractive and objectionable. From housekeeping to child-rearing, including her appearance and taste in clothes; even her few gray hairs. No longer could she do anything right to please him in any way.

The largest issue for her was that he had sudden outbursts in which he lashed out in phrases like, "you always…" and "you never..." When she asked him to tell her how he would like things to be, his response was, "If I must tell you, you're not good enough for me."

A very talented, sensitive, and intelligent man, Zach could out-argue anyone. His "one-upmanship" was honed to a fine art. He was never "wrong." After so many years, she knew that *talking things over* when there were two sides to an issue was not his way. She had to be left in the penitent's position at the end.

As she had arranged, the cab was waiting in the morning. Zachary was there with his suitcase. The couple put their luggage in the trunk and stepped into the backseat from opposite sides. Zach confirmed the airport destination with the driver, and the taxi started on its way.

They hadn't exchanged a single word and sat as far away from one another as they could, staring straight ahead, each wrapped in private musings. In the thick silence that engulfed her, thoughts tripping over each other in her brain, a gleam of hope appeared in the fact that he was there. He kept his commitment to go. The threat was bluster. That was a first tiny step to a way out of this ugly stand-off in which he had landed them. There was no conversation all the way to the airport and only a few necessary words after to pay the driver and to read the signs to the correct departure gate.

Two strangers married to each other arrived in Bermuda a few hours later. Rebecca felt more comfortable being in a place where no one knew them and would notice their glum expressions and lack of communication. In the crowded hotel elevator, they heard their name called from the rear. Oops! All this way from home there *was* someone there who did. It was one of Zach's students and her mother. They came on the same plane. He introduced Rebecca appropriately and they went to their rooms.

The lovely beach of fine powdery white sand made pink by tiny bits of red coral, the sky of intense cobalt blue, and the deep turquoise of the sea were balm to her aching soul. They toured, walked the beach and the town, and investigated shops; they dined in the luxurious surroundings of the hotel restaurant. Conversation was sparse, centered on the immediate present. They concentrated on verbal interactions remarking on the beauty and huge size of the plants that grew outdoors, while at home they had to be nurtured in small pots, the incredible turquoise hue of the water, and blue of the sky. She commented on the traffic and the interesting ways the Bermudians conserve rainwater by tiers on the roofs that collect the drops and channel them to a cistern at the corner of the buildings.

The permanently scarring wringer Zach had put her through was not mentioned nor did he speak of the demons that were propelling his imagination to become so inflamed. Rebecca was hoping that in this relaxing, colorful environment with no domestic pressures he would open up and tell her honestly what was gnawing at his soul. It didn't happen.

Zach was polite and appeared calm and neutral; Rebecca was thankful for the momentary cessation of hostility, still holding out a hope that miraculously this mutual experience would lead to a more peaceful partnership in the future.

A few minutes after their arrival at home it was as if they had never been away. Zach's temper flared over the slightest things. Disappointed, Rebecca realized that this was to be her life. She had no professional skills to offer in the labor market to provide for her children, nor the self-confidence to go it on her own. If she were to stay she had to accommodate by toughening her sensitivities and to manage his bullying. To leave meant an uncertain economic future to which she didn't intend to subject the children. Time passed, and life went on, between tantrums.

AN INSIGHT

Picture a cloudy, foggy day in the parking lot of a shopping center. I was busy loading the filled paper bags of groceries into the trunk of my borrowed Volvo not aware of what was going on in the background of my brain. Determined to back out of the tight parking space without a fender bender, I put the gear shift in reverse, glanced in the rear-view mirror to make sure no one was there, checked the sides, stepped on the gas lightly, and had that momentary dizzy sensation I always get when moving backward. I was especially careful in the dull lighting of this soggy day.

In that instant, before I was done backing out, an image of two parallel lines, like railroad tracks that never meet, even at the furthest horizon appeared on my mental screen. It was a graphic way to visualize or perhaps it's better to say crystallize and accept my thorny problem regarding religious faith and the stories that go with it, versus the rationalism of science.

I had been in emotional turmoil about this for years, and now it was suddenly clear. That image helped integrate these two poles with which I was having such a difficult time, into what felt to be a reasonably comfortable equilibrium. It was like the saying, "East is east, and West is west, and never the twain shall meet." They don't need to meet, they run parallel. Seeing it this way became all right for me. It was a great relief to reconcile these issues, although it seemed to be a strange place and time for such a startling revelation.

This was a moment of significance on my journey. My memory jumped back to my first contact with the concept of a deity that came by way of my grandmother when I was five. It was soon after the beginning of WWII. My family had been deported to a remote settlement in Siberia and we kids were playing outdoors when I was hit by a rock tossed by a boy.

My forehead was bleeding what seemed like buckets and I ran to Grandma very frightened. She laid me down, put a cool cloth on my head while telling my sobbing self that I had to forgive the boy and that God would take care of any punishment He thought necessary. She said that I had to forgive, or God would be angry with me. I thought about that for a while but wasn't convinced. In time, my wound healed, and I didn't pay any more attention to the matter.

Later that year, Grandma found that I had been slicing and eating thin slivers from the salami left on the table one evening while the adults were out. I tried to deny it. Again, she spoke about God. She said, "God sees everything and knows everything; he also knows all your thoughts". That was scary but didn't have much effect on the practical aspects of my life. I was too busy being five years old, dealing with the realities of hunger, frostbite on my fingers, and imagining as reality what my friend Valia was telling me of the golden streets in Moscow.

My more earnest efforts to bring sense into my personal belief system must have begun around the age of twelve. At that time, my family had arrived in America. I was enrolled in a Talmud Torah, the religious school of a Sephardic Synagogue. I had very scant knowledge of English and not much interest in the additional hours in a school room. Before that, I had not experienced a religious education as most of my peers in American school did, because I was attending school in the Soviet Union during the reign of Joseph Stalin at a time and place where a belief in the supernatural was anathema, seen as a criminal offense.

The moment on that rainy day in the parking lot was a significant few seconds. It gave a new perspective to the matter of science and religion in my personal scheme of things.

A REMARKABLE MAN

On the morning of the first meeting of a Road Scholar program the group gathered for a holiday tour of San Diego, I noticed a blind man and his wife. His name was Joe. I was struck by his lively participation in conversation with people on both sides of him at the table. I admired his confident, easy ability to engage verbally on any subject with total strangers.

While sightseeing, he consistently kept up with the group as we got on and off the coach, his arm always linked to his wife Debbie's. He asked pertinent questions and made interesting comments that showed that he knew a great deal about many things. I was curious how he could manage the deep engagement and curiosity despite such a serious handicap and how it came about. I wondered if he had been born sightless or if that befell him later in life. In the days that followed I had occasional opportunity for brief conversations with this awesome couple but didn't ask.

Eventually he told the story. He was a practicing pediatrician in Portland, Oregon, when a heart problem required that he undergo surgery. Something went desperately wrong with the anesthesia. When he came to his sight was gone.

Within the same year his wife died. Later he married a long-time family friend who seems to have an enormous capacity for giving and being understanding. They travel as often as they can, doing it with dignity and remarkable energy.

Joe is a captivating man; his sense of humor and interest in everything is inspiring. At the special dinner on New Year's Eve, I was seated at the same table as Joe and his wife. When the music began, he swept her elegantly onto the dance floor and they kept perfect pace with the other couples. After escorting her back to the table, he asked some of the other women to dance. He carried it off as if he were a much younger, sighted swain, chatting casually while gliding around the small dance floor between the tables.

We enjoyed our conversations, and on parting expressed a mutual hope that our paths would cross again. On my sweep through Portland on another tour that meeting didn't work out, but I still hope another time it will. San Diego is an exciting city to see, but meeting Joseph and Debbie was definitely a highlight of that tour.

A SEARCH WITHOUT AN END (so far)

Since my arrival at Pier 57 in New York City 64 years ago, I continue my pursuit of the emotional comfort of feeling that someone (or two) understands.

Thus far, this magic prize has eluded me and so the quest continues. My assumption that the attainment of certain educational or creative goals would allow me entry to feelings of the emotional security of being part of the social environment may be unrealistic, a fantasy.

Yes, there were moments along the way when I thought, "Now I've got it, I'm finally *home*." These moments were brief, and they passed to leave me feeling on the *outside* repeatedly. What is the feeling I'm striving for? Is there such a thing as a sense of comfort within a group that anyone has? I don't know.

Not one of my acquaintances understands what I mean when I say, "I'm looking for someone who speaks *my language*." It's difficult to explain the lack of a sense of rootedness, of history, to those who can trace their families back a generation or two or more, and have many collective memories, or the survivors of WWII who are older and don't accept me as one of *them* because I'm younger.

In fact, it's so difficult that I have lived the last 70 years without encountering such a soul. I have made-do, and done quite well, judging by accepted social standards and appearances.

I was a good student, passed through the appropriate life cycle activities expected of a girl: I married, made a home, had children, raised them, let them go out into the world. I have accomplished a modicum educationally - two MS degrees - and artistically as a painter, have been widowed twice, built friendships, traveled, and did other things. All the while, I have also been searching for that person or several people with whom I can feel truly *at home*.

My American-born first husband had no clue. At that time, it was the custom to say, "It's over, forget it," about what one may have experienced during the war. He had no desire to put himself in my shoes to try and understand me. He disapproved of what may have been my left-over issues after the excitement of what he probably thought of as exotic wore off.

My late, Brooklyn-born second husband understood me better than anyone ever has, despite his German heritage and different religious tradition.

Imagine the emotional turmoil and disappointment when I was invited to attend a gathering in Manhattan, New York, of hidden children that survived the Holocaust. I protested because I wasn't a hidden child. The Drs. Kestenbaum, who were engaged in a study of survivors urged me to come.

"We're looking for people like you" they said. They asked where I had spent the war years. I told them clearly that we were in a Siberian labor camp and, later, a collective farm in Uzbekistan. They urged me to come and I went.

I left that encounter feeling far worse than any before or since. The people at that meeting took away my legitimacy in a few sentences.

"Why are you here?"

"You think you suffered? You don't know anything about suffering."

"You don't really belong here."

It was suggested that I had no business considering myself a *survivor* and attending such a meeting.

In self-defense, I said that I didn't know I was in a competition to see who suffered the most and left the meeting feeling humiliated and embarrassed, like an interloper. I had expected something quite different; the experience of that afternoon left a deep scar.

Over time, in many a discussion when the subject comes up, I hear the declaration, "Oh, forget it, you're too sensitive."

Lately, for the first time, I have formed a response to that insinuation and judgment. "Who appointed the judges to decide what the standard of sensitivity has to be?" I think it's an important thought to keep in mind on such occasions.

Another time I felt more than uncomfortable relating to the issue of survival was at a candle-lighting ceremony for the "six million" at my temple in Westchester County, New York. At my husband's insistence, because I was too shy, I joined the group on the bima and lighted one of the six candles. Afterward, some members of the congregation chided me, saying, "Why did you go up to light a candle? You weren't part of the Holocaust." These people knew nothing about me and didn't ask. They felt free to decide that I had usurped a position of honor to which I was not entitled. Thus, I was denied the sense of being part of the group again.

This happening in addition to the fact that I don't bring a sense of belonging to the table, wasn't particularly helpful to my self-confidence. As said before, I have learned to live a productive, creative, and often enjoyable life in spite of the lack of emotional kinship.

I have heard of an organization of survivors in the city to which I moved. My one opportunity for an encounter with them was a dismal failure. The same attitude of 'superior suffering' emanated from this gathering as I had experienced years ago in New York. They showed no interest at all in my joining their ranks. May be this happens because I'm younger than most of the members of this group and am seen by them as having been 'only a child,' with no feeling or impressionability worthy of consideration. My damaged psyche, lack of childhood, and remembered deprivations don't factor in. In their scheme of things, the trauma of a child, which I was then, doesn't carry weight equal to their suffering and can be dismissed.

And we talk about Brotherhood. I thought it started at home. Bah! Humbug!

A WORD PICTURE
January 1, 2011

The rains have stopped.
Muddy patches dot the trail showing
dog-paw and sneaker prints in the soft brown earth.
It's New Year's Day under a clear, brilliant blue sky.
Not even a trace of cloud can be seen,
only two white, silently lengthening contrails
very high in the sky.
Close by, boulders piled in what looks like
haphazard formations
sit in the ground along the gently curving hills
on freshly-carpeted vivid yellow-green earth,
the aftermath of recent torrential downpours.
A young couple with a bright-eyed little girl
in a pink dress and a slender black dog on a
leash are strolling on the trail.
Black grebes with snow-white beaks
float along foraging busily among the reeds.
A few white egrets sit on the water in the
distant part of the lake.
An occasional chirp-a-chirp trill of a bird
breaks the stillness
over the silver streaked lake under the sun.
The quietude of this noon time lulls the rough
edges of the rest of the world
literally falling apart at this very instant.
The most cruel, unwinnable wars in history
are being waged,
most likely with dismal outcomes
for all the combatants.
I drink in the peace and loveliness of the moment.
I'll think about that another time.

AT THE FLAT IRON BUILDING

One cold and dreary winter evening in January 1956, I had made a date with a new acquaintance to meet in the lobby of the Flatiron Building in New York City. The plan was to go from there to dinner at one of the many Indian restaurants on 23rd Street.

The building, a landmark sits on a triangular property at the intersection of Fifth Avenue and Broadway, between 22nd and 23rd Streets. At 20 stories high, it was one of the tallest when it was completed in 1902. Its name comes from its resemblance to the wedge shape of the cast iron clothes-pressing appliances of the time.

The lobby of this building would provide a convenient meeting spot, given that we each took a different subway line to get there. If either of us was early, waiting there would be more comfortable than on the cold, dark street in New York in January.

I arrived at the appointed place, pushed the opening of the revolving door entrance and was glad of the welcoming warmth and bright lights in the lobby. I waited for what seemed many minutes, then began to pace the length of the corridor. Being of a worrying nature, I wondered what might have happened, and called home to ask my mother if my date-to-be had called. She said yes, he had. The message was that he was at the building waiting and concerned why I had not appeared. I continued to walk around to keep my impatience under control, and noticed that there were two exits/entrances, both with revolving doors.

He was most likely looking for me at the other door and we were missing each other every time we made the circuit. Hungry and exasperated by what seemed an unending cycle, I stopped making the rounds, and stayed in place to wait, hoping to intercept him the next time my anxious-looking swain came that way. It worked. Good thing was that that we didn't know one another very well at that point, or the encounter might have been much less polite than it was.

Six months later, we stood under a wedding canopy, and the fateful date at the Flatiron Building was never mentioned again.

AUDREY'S BIRTHDAY PARTY

Audrey is having a pool party for her birthday.

I was invited, along with her great grandfather, my neighbor/friend. He and I represent the generation of great grandparents; it's a new designation for me, I have no great-grandkids.

A black Lab mix named Dexter that likes to greet by putting his paws on people's shoulders, and Ashley, a slobbering brown Boxer welcome us as we step from the vehicle. They sniff, lick our hands, and walk away. We deliver our gifts to Audrey's mom, to be added to the collection with the others to be opened later and are led to two chairs in the shade at the edge of the pool. Of all the people there, I know only my friend's son, his wife, and his grandson.

My friend and I settle in, I begin to look around to get a sense of where I am. The house feels secluded, one boundary is a line of tall live oak trees; a park. Very nice.

The little girls from three to ten or eleven years old in two-piece swimsuits, their long hair matted from the water and the boys in brightly patterned longish swim trunks are jumping up and down in and out of the water, tossing balloons decorated with emoji faces at each other, squealing with delight, and laughing; frolicking as befits the happy occasion. The children have unusual names: Axel, Brinley, Adelie. Wyatt.

Food is set out under the building's overhang to keep it in the shade. There's a package of crackers and dips in containers, hamburgers and hot dogs are on a plate, buns in a package next to them. Sliced tomatoes, onions and lettuce leaves are on other plates, and a bottle each of mustard and catchup is available. I offer to bring my handicapped friend some lunch. There are no serving utensils, only my fingers to use to put dip on the crackers, the hamburger into the bun, and to lift the lettuce, tomato, etc. A keg of beer and paper cups are within easy reach.

We sit in the cool shade delighting in watching the children frolic in the pool and jump on the trampoline. It's very entertaining and we admire the unbounded amounts of energy they have. The twelve of them get along remarkably well; there is friendly competition diving, tossing balls and other things; no fights, no hurt feelings, no complaints, and no tears. Amazing how joyously they get along.

As a people-watcher, I also observe the parents who are the generation of our grandchildren, and occasionally comment to my friend on my impressions. I don't recognize myself as a younger adult as I look at these folks. It's strange. The women are likely in the thirties and up. Their hair is long and hanging on both sides of the face and down the back. Frequently they pass their fingers through it to fluff it or tie it in a knot that comes apart immediately. It continues to fall into their face. Their shirts have cut-outs at the shoulders and back, the better to display tattoos that cover the skin on those areas. They cover the lower parts of their bodies in Capri pants or shorts with more tattoos visible on ankles and calves. On their feet flip-flops of varying degrees of expense protect their soles from harm, some are encrusted with sparkling "jewels" to expose the tattoos on their feet. The ladies sit chatting in a circle under an umbrella; I hope they are keeping an eye out for the children running around and in the pool.

The men are equally formal in backward-turned baseball caps, sunglasses, sleeveless t-shirts, shorts, and flip-flops. They play a lawn game, talk shop, laugh, and look contented masticating the refreshments and drinking beer.

Hanging out poolside, idly watching the children and adults, I make some involuntary observations and suppositions about one of the men. His head is shaved, and a long straggly beard that he caresses often hangs from his chin. He is probably in his forties. He wears a sleeveless t-shirt with lettering on the front, floppy shorts, and flip-flops. He is the only person in the company that lights and smokes cigarettes on site. There's something unsavory about him. He hugs one of the older girls in a way I find uncomfortable and am surprised to see that she responds positively. I hear later that the girl is his daughter, that he is the irresponsible brother of the hostess, a non-working moocher and con man. It seems my observation is on target.

The kids are playing in the pool and doing somersaults on the trampoline for hours with no diminishing energy; the two dogs patrol for scraps and sit at our feet when we eat, watching with their soulful eyes for a possible handout. It's a joyous scene.

The sun moves on, it gets chilly, the hostess wraps a blanket around me. How sweet! The children continue to run, dive, and jump, but we two fossils are ready to go home.

COUSINS / SISTERS

In the summer of 1939, my cousin Elise was three and a half years old. She lived with my aunt and uncle in a lovely villa on the edge of Bielsko, a city in southwestern Poland. While her parents were on vacation in France for a month, her grandparents and nanny were providing loving care, and Bella, a belly-to-the-ground reddish-brown dachshund, was there for company.

On September first, Hitler's armies invaded the country and overran Poland in several days.

To be out of harm's way, the grandparents dismissed the nanny and fled east with their little granddaughter hoping to find safety in the town of Kolomea. While my aunt and uncle were away, the German Chancellor Adolph Hitler signed a non-aggression pact with Joseph Stalin, the head of the Soviet Union, in which he promised not to invade the giant to the east. He didn't keep his word and Russia was invaded. In the general confusion that resulted, my aunt and uncle could not return from France, my cousin and her grandparents became political prisoners of the Soviets, as did my family and millions of others throughout Poland and neighboring countries. In their case, they were loaded onto cattle cars and transported east to Bodaybo, a small town in eastern Siberia in the province of Irkutsk.

Caught up in the same worldwide tempest, my parents and I were picked up in Lvov, a Polish city founded in the 13th century bordering Ukraine, and were deported east by the Soviets. With no means of communication, each family was unaware of the other's whereabouts.

Our destination turned out to be the Republic of Yakutia, a vast area of northern Siberia. After fifteen months, including a winter of unimaginable cold and starvation we were "liberated" from that middle of nowhere place of the world, and allowed to travel within the Soviet Union, with the strict proviso that we were not to settle in cities. Despite limits on our options, my mother was determined to leave the frigid climate, to go somewhere more temperate. On the way south the military intervened, diverting our course, this time to Uzbekistan in Central Asia.

Thanks to the word-of-mouth network that always seemed to come to life in times of chaos and mass confusion, my mother discovered that my cousin and her grandparents were also deported – to the Republic of Irkutsk, in Southern Siberia

She conceived the notion of bringing Elise and her grandparents Alex and Agatha to live with us, in the belief that being cousins only nine months apart in age, we would benefit by growing up together as if we were sisters. I was thrilled with the prospect of having a playmate and confidante and could hardly wait for Elise to join us.

It was a long wait, allowing me plenty of time to develop fantasies about the wonderful time to come into almost tangible realities.

Months later, my parents welcomed Agatha, Alex, and Elise into our one-room clay brick home on a collective farm. To accommodate them and make them comfortable, we moved our belongings around to occupy only half the space and invited them to use the other half. We shared our food and introduced them to the local way of life on a farm in Central Asia. I was thrilled to be part of a larger family. It was more like the ones I saw around me.

My parents' meager earnings were not enough to feed six. Agatha and Alex were in good health and able to work. After some weeks, my parents requested that they contribute to the welfare of the family unit or make their own arrangements; particularly so as my parents were not related to Agatha and Alex.

They were my cousin's maternal relatives yet considered themselves entitled to full support by my father, as if he were their son. They claimed the entitlement based on their greater age. That was not in sync with what my mother envisioned. Her thinking was along lines of cooperation to make the stressful conditions of wartime more bearable by being together. My folks were in no position to adopt a family.

Conflicts began to surface. Tensions grew between the adults, simmering just below a layer of civility, occasionally erupting in loud arguments about food and housekeeping issues. Sometimes my father said angry things. When the grownups had a confrontation, he seemed like a stranger to me, not the warm, kind, and self-sacrificing person that I loved and respected. I wanted to hide when my parents had to defend their lives and mine from people they themselves had invited into our home. It wasn't right. The loud outbursts were upsetting, and their bitter memory lingered.

My relationship with Elise was affected, it wasn't what I had hoped for; deeply disappointing. We were not like sisters at all.

Grandmother Agatha was a very spirited, bright, and imaginative lady. She told amusing, entertaining stories to us kids, and invented malignant tales with no basis in truth about my parents' sources of income and connections, frequently insinuating that she and her husband were unfairly treated. She set Elise and the kids we played with against me by making fun of the way I walked, the way I talked and took things too seriously. I was too slow a runner and she encouraged the kids to tease me mercilessly.

These insults hurt, and I complained to my mother, who was always very polite, unwilling to engage in a quarrel or any possibly disagreeable verbal exchange. She tried to pretend it wasn't happening, counseling me to ignore these slights, "Just walk away." Easier said than done at an age when these things matter so much.

Elise was brave, brash, and athletic – a tomboy; whereas I was cautious and quiet, trained to household chores and 'girl' things. When we played outdoors, she thought nothing of climbing up to the roof of a barn and jumping down into a pile of straw, challenging everybody else to follow. She did it repeatedly, enjoying every jump. I watched with admiration and perhaps a touch of envy but wouldn't even make the attempt to climb way up there. When we went swimming, she took running leaps into a fast-moving irrigation canal and swam as if she were born in it; I was terrified to jump even from the edge. With grandma's encouragement, some kids pushed me in, and I did my panicky best paddling for dear life to get out. I still have a scar on my arm where an underwater tree branch or root ripped my skin as I fell in.

In school, books and supplies were a rarity. The only blank paper that existed was on the back of portraits of Stalin in propaganda booklets; unfortunately to use those to write on was an official crime against the state. It would be awful to be banished to the snows of

Siberia for such a transgression. Any blank scrap of paper and pencil stub was hard to come by and treasured when found; its use was stretched as much as possible.

One day we came home with our report cards. I had all fives, the highest grade, and felt good about being in the top of the class. My cousin had fours on her document.

Without a word grandmother grabbed Elise, laid her bottom-up across her lap, pulled down her underpants, and administered a thorough spanking for not having achieved equally well. I was shocked and took on a burden of guilt, feeling that I caused the situation by doing so well. It took all my happy feelings out of me; I reasoned that if I hadn't been such a good student this wouldn't have happened. Elise didn't tell me how she felt about it, but an unspoken barrier came between us. We were not friends. She liked to run and climb and dare, I was quiet and enjoyed learning academic things. The grandmother was pitting us against one another.

When sides for a team game were being chosen, I was the last one to be called.

In the summer we wore only undies; no tops, no socks, no shoes. We didn't have any.

By age ten, I was beginning to show signs of feminine development. Grandma had a whole new vein of teasing material to mine; she used it cleverly to make me thoroughly and miserably self-conscious. Soon every part of our life was filled with conflicts and arguments. Elise and I bickered about everything. Sitting across from each other at meals, we argued endlessly. Her grandfather threatened to build what he called a "Chinese" wall between us to have some peace at mealtime. I didn't know about the Great Wall of China then.

When I was sick, which was more often than my cousin, Agatha taunted me surreptitiously when my mother wasn't there, implying that I was playacting and malingering. When I had serious fevers, she called me an unworthy weakling. Despite admiring her playfulness and generally cheerful disposition, I liked her less and less; in fact, I detested her. One day I said, "I hate her." My mother said I mustn't hate anybody, but in this case, it was hard.

Living in one room and having every word 'interpreted' and every act criticized day after day was very challenging.

An issue that has had deep repercussions for me was the grandfather's firmly held notion, that in any difference of opinion I had to cede. Constant reminders that I was the older one (by nine months), and 'should know better' than being selfish and want my way annoyed me. On the other hand, I was exhorted, "You're young, and should respect and obey your elders." I was always the 'older' or the 'younger'; there was no time with this man when I counted just because I was.

Unfortunately, my mother's brilliant idea to improve our lives by having a full family with a sister and grandparents was more painful and problematic in ways she had not foreseen in her worst nightmares.

In time, a tiny room, no bigger than a walk-in closet became vacant at the other end of the clay brick structure. To retain some part of our sanity and outlook, my mother convinced the farmyard foreman to let us live in it. It was so tiny, that my father had to go back to our original room to sleep for the night. It was a blessing to have this little haven out of Agatha's earshot and line of vision; it eliminated some of the clashes about what food belongs to whom, and mealtime squabbling between us girls. We were grateful for the peace this change brought to our threesome.

The war in Europe was declared over when Elise and I were in our eleventh year. When the opportunity came, the family opted to be repatriated to our hometown in Poland.

The journey back was two weeks filled with the joyful expectation of going 'home' in spite of doing it in a cattle car again.

On arrival, we finally went our separate ways. Our former home was intact but occupied by Poles who were very vocal in expressing their disappointment and anger that we had survived. We managed to locate temporary quarters, a room in a Polish family's apartment including grudging bath and toilet privileges.

It took many months for my mother and me to become emotionally cleansed of the poison that had settled in our system over time, living with the chronic level of high anxiety; the spying and the unhealthy preoccupations that had sunk into our souls were destructive. My father didn't express his feelings on the subject.

In Polish school Elise and I were assigned to the same class and were seated at adjoining desks. Later in Stockholm, waiting for a quota number to immigrate to America we were housed at the same hotel at Normalmstorg Number 4. At least we were no longer living in the same room.

During the winter of 1947, papers came through allowing Elise and her grandparents to leave for the U.S. She was reunited with her parents seven long years after they left for what was expected to be a month.

My aunt and uncle survived the war, settled in New York, and had another baby in 1945.

When Big Sister Elise arrived, she had no idea how to fit into the family. She was quite unprepared to take her place as the older sibling with people who were complete strangers. In addition to that she didn't know the language (English) her parents and baby sister were speaking.

Those first few years must have been very difficult. Her mother didn't seem to understand that this girl was not sent to her to be a maid or nanny, but her own child. Despite it all Elise made an excellent adjustment. She attended the local school in a town outside New York City, and continued to New York University, even winning a coveted Fulbright Scholarship.

My knowledge of her life in the U.S. is sketchy, gathered and inferred from conversations with her sister, a woman who became a good friend to me in our old age. Elise and I have had very few personal contacts in the ensuing sixty years. They were limited to attending my uncle's funeral in 1954, Elise's marriage ceremony in 1955, and in 1956, my wedding. None of those interactions resulted in our re-connecting. She was financially comfortable, independent, ambitious, moving into the future. I worked as a textile colorist, was married to a scientist, and we scrimped to make 'ends meet.' Given our background, living in different economic worlds, and being of such different temperaments, blood ties weren't enough to motivate us to cultivate a personal relationship.

In the 1960s, my cousin and I crossed paths at a reception for her mother's ceramics exhibit. She was on the arm of a short older man I had never seen; not the tall, young man I had met at her wedding.

"Hello Ruth, how nice of you and Gerry to come. This is my husband Joseph." I was taken aback; no one ever told me. It appears that in the interim she had two children, divorced, became a Spanish teacher, and married the chairman of the language department at her high school. This was the man she introduced at the exhibit. After that evening, she disappeared from my life again.

Our next encounter was at the end of August 1976, during a short condolence visit on the death of my husband Gerry. We walked in the neighborhood park enjoying the warmth of the waning rays of a sunny day.

"We must have lunch one of these days soon, call me," she said when we parted, but failed to give me her number. I thought she meant to get together. I learned that it's a phrase commonly used quite without sincerity to terminate a meeting graciously.

Seventeen more years passed. I invited my recently returned from many years in Florida aunt to the opening reception of a solo exhibition of my paintings at a library gallery. When I called her, she said, "I heard that you got married. Who's the lucky guy? I'd like to meet him. You'll introduce me when I come to see your show, okay? And I'll bring Elise and Connie, too. By the way, Connie married into a large, wealthy family."

In the brief phone conversation, I also learned that Elise married for a third time after yet another divorce; that she dropped the teaching profession and became an industrialist–owner/operator of a manufacturing and retail business of women's clothing. She and her new husband owned several stores on prime real estate in Manhattan - corners of Madison Avenue in the eighties, and often traveled to Europe to the fashion shows. What amazing energy and stamina she has! I thought.

When she appeared at the door of the gallery, I recognized her instantly by her smile unmistakably Grandma Agatha's. Skeletally skinny, clad in close-fitting black, her dyed brown hair was fashionably clipped to half-inch length with a bleached white patch in front. She was far more stylish than the crowd of casually dressed suburbanites at this party. I was momentarily at a loss for words but recovered while moving forward to welcome her.

"How good to see you again! It's been a long, long time!" I gushed while taking in her fashion-plate image, and no doubt comparing it with my own softer, rounder, less dramatic appearance.

"What are you doing these days?" I asked as an opener.

"Building an empire… What about you?" She answered without hesitation grinning with satisfaction.

"What you see on these walls." I answered with a sweeping gesture to indicate several dozen works hanging on the wall around the room. Feeling very small and the 'poor relative' once again, I wished I could say something equally grandiose about my activities.

"Where is your husband?" She asked in an interrogatory manner, as if ticking off a mental check list. Before I could look around to locate him, she continued, "What does he do? I want to meet him."

I had sensed that the motivation of my three relatives to attend this reception was sheer curiosity, not in the slightest bit connected to my artistic effort or accomplishment. I led her to Robert and introduced him to her. She looked him up and down, made a quick appraisal, and she and I continued our stroll around the room for a few more minutes looking at the paintings and photographs, exchanging inane remarks about aging gracefully.

Suddenly, she stopped, turned to me, and said, "You were always the talented one," in a tone that sounded wistful and made me wonder if it's an ability that perhaps she would have liked to own too. What was she thinking? I never found out.

Their curiosity satisfied, my aunt, Elise, and Connie departed not to be heard from again for many years. The extent of our interactions continued to be minimal, although with increasing age there seemed to be a softening in attitudes toward one another. I no longer felt the sharp enmity and competitiveness with her.

Looking back on the decades that have gone, I think perhaps our talents and temperaments were such that we were not destined to be what I would have liked us to be, friends and family. It seemed that

Elise had put her past behind her, never referred to it. For me, it has never been absent, and continues to be an influence in shaping my world view.

DINNER COUPON

A stoop-shouldered elderly man wearing a shirt with sleeves rolled up, and sagging pants that look as if they belong on a larger person, shuffles into a steak restaurant late one afternoon. His long rectangular face, brooding, heavy-lidded eyes, and sad demeanor elicit a sense of sympathy for the "poor guy" from anyone who notices him. There's something tragic in that hangdog look.

The manager recognizes him and ushers him to the spot by a window where he likes to sit. He has been here before to have an early-bird dinner and presents a newspaper coupon for an additional discount. He orders his meal and a glass of red wine. Between sips of wine and bites of his steak and potatoes, he reads the daily paper. A man with very small capacity for food, he beckons the server when he has eaten his fill: "Would you please bring me a box to take the rest of this home?"

She returns quickly, "Here you are Sir."

He transfers the leftovers into the container, closes it carefully, and places it into a plastic bag; his mission is accomplished. He has enough left over to eat for the next two nights. While tying the two handles on the bag together he's calculating how he will apportion its contents at home over the next two dinners and will only want to add a glass of wine to make the meal complete. He relaxes a little longer watching through the window as people in the parking lot go about their business, while he finishes his wine. When he empties the glass he's ready to leave.

At the register, he extends his credit card to the cashier. "It's all right Sir," she says waving it away, "your dinner is already paid for, thank you for stopping by."

"Who paid for it?" Lester asks but she won't tell.

Why? Is it a PR gesture on the part of management for being a repeat customer? Is it another guest?

Eight months later the same thing happens. The question remains.

FACE-BODY DISCONNECT

Recently, I passed a full-length mirror in a country club and caught sight of my reflection. I thought, "How ironic it is that that very thing happened to me."

This is what happened: I entered the social worker's office of an assisted living/nursing home facility with my 86-year-old mother for an interview. A strikingly pretty, young woman greeted us with a brilliant smile of welcome from her seat behind a large desk crowded with folders and the paraphernalia that used to inhabit office desktops before the paperless and pen-less society overtook us. She extended her arms inviting us to have a seat in the two chairs opposite her. She was professional, well-spoken, and gentle in her approach. My Mom answered questions regarding her past, and her present living arrangements at my home, and some other pertinent matters to assess whether she was a potential candidate for the facility; her responses were polite, clear, and succinct. Then came what to me was the key question.

"How would you like to live here?"

"Absolutely not!" was the answer in a voice as resolute and definite as anyone would want to hear. If she could have spoken in bold capital letters she would have.

My heart sank. What would I do now? This was the pivotal event that would determine her future and mine. As undemanding and pleasant as my mother was, I could no longer cope with her physical needs on my own at home. My attempt to hire a caregiver through an agency was a disaster that made me not want to try again. They sent an obviously deranged applicant. I lost all trust in the notion of leaving my mother at home with anyone even for an hour. Assisted living in a facility was the only possible reasonably safe option.

We were getting ready to take a look-around, to walk through the facility. The pretty social worker hoisted herself from her chair and came around from behind the desk that had till now blocked her lower half from view.

Her beautiful face was a mismatch to the big fleshy hips and bulky body she carried on heavy legs. The thought, "I hope never to look like that," crossed my mind.

When I saw the above-mentioned reflection, it reminded me of that moment years ago. How disappointing! I think apologies to that pretty social worker every time I catch a glimpse of myself in a mirror.

FLAT TIRE

While backing out of my parking space I hear an unfamiliar new sound coming from somewhere in my car. It follows me the two miles on the drive to my destination. I hear it again on the way home.

I check for any loose object in the trunk and the glove compartment but find nothing. A few minutes later my husband arrives; I lean out the driver's window to greet him. A shadow of distress clouds his usually friendly face.

"You better get on the phone," he says, "and get somebody here right away to fix your tire."

"My tire?" I ask incredulously. "What's wrong with it?"

"Don't you look at your tires before you drive?" There's a hint of remonstrance in his voice.

I am waiting for AAA to arrive. In an unusual twist in the weather, it's raining. The female voice on the cell phone informs me that the man whose mission it is to help me can't find the address. While explaining directions to her, I notice a very large flat-bed truck lumbering up the long driveway of our development. I wave to the driver in hopes of being noticed.

The vehicle looks too cumbersome to negotiate the tight curve to get to my car. It makes it. I am so glad to see my rescuer, but despite my waving efforts he doesn't seem to see me, and it looks like he may leave.

I tell the lady on the phone; she reassures me. "He hung up, so he sees you."

Still not acknowledging that he saw me, he stops the vehicle and swings the door open. Out steps a huge bulky man with disheveled reddish hair, an enormous pot-belly, and a mass of tattoos peeking out from under his shirt. I feel very small, somewhat like I might feel if I were confronting the Giant in Jack and the Beanstalk, or meeting Paul Bunyan. He is wearing a greasy black baseball-style cap, its peak adorned with flame-shaped designs of yellow and bright red. His shirt buttons are straining the buttonholes across his voluminous torso, and his beard and mustache needed a trim some time ago.

He makes some contemptuous-sounding observations, none of which I understand. I assume they have something to do with the foul weather. I listen very attentively and try to separate the sounds he's making into distinct words. After all, he's here on a mission of mercy for my punctured tire.

Robert is standing by for moral and practical support, should it become necessary. From his body language and the grunts he utters, we gather the driver wants to know where the lug nut to unlock the hubcap is stored. We lift the cover off the spare tire to see if it's there. He reaches in confidently, and in one deft move finds exactly what he needs. Relief….

Now he gets down to the real business of jacking the car up, folding his bulky body down to the ground. In a moment, the car is lifted, the sick tire is removed, the spare put on and tightened, the car is lowered, and the operation is complete. Robert says something; they both laugh (probably each at his own cleverness).

In response to Robert's question, we find out where the tire with a deeply imbedded ten-penny nail in it can be repaired. A few more smiles, unintelligible remarks, and the angel of mercy to tires is on his way to the next call with an extra ten-dollar bill in his pocket.

Someone famous once said, "All's well that ends well."

You bet!!!

FULL MOON

A slender arc of orange peeks from
behind the mountain in the dusky darkening sky.
Quickly it climbs in the indigo firmament,
revealing its full roundness.
Smaller now to the earthbound eye,
its color a whitened yellow,
it emits a glowing light to display
the nocturnal landscape of a clear night.
The full moon.

HANDSHAKE

When I think of merging into traffic on one of California's congested fast-moving freeways, my palms become cold and clammy in response to the stress of the anticipation of the move. That instant always reminds me of many decades ago when the symptom plagued me and caused me to feel self-conscious and awkward every time I thought I might meet a new person in a social situation.

In my earlier life in Central Asia the western ritual of shaking hands wasn't part of the greeting ceremony. In that part of the world in the early 1940s, there was no need or opportunity for my parents to teach me that specific ritual. Women there embraced in greeting while saying a version of "Salaam." As a pre-teen girl, that did not apply to me.

When I was 13 years old, shortly after our arrival in the United States, I was being introduced to a man. He proffered his hand and probably noticed my hesitation.

"Aren't you going to shake my hand?" he asked.

I didn't know exactly what to do so I mimicked his movement and stretched mine toward him, doing what I saw people do when greeting each other. I extended my smaller, instantly clammy hand to him.

"Your handshake is like a dead fish," he reacted with disgust in his voice. "You'd better change that fast if you want to be liked." I was aghast, and I admit indelibly intimidated by the fact that I was making such a bad impression.

I secretly carried my sense of inadequacy when confronted by having to make manual contact in greeting with me, and tried to avoid encounters where that type of activity was necessary. In our society, the shaking of hands is a very common accepted practice, a form of greeting one another at all levels of social interaction. It originates far back in time when the convention developed to show that one was unarmed and intended no bodily harm upon meeting. Since usually the right hand would have held the cudgel or other implement, that's customarily the hand that we proffer in peaceable, friendly greeting.

I told my father what had happened, and how mortified I was when someone offered me a hand to shake. He said, "We'll fix that." He taught me to extend my arm and take the other person's hand with a firm, confident grasp, follow it by a brief series of up and down movements while expressing verbal gladness to meet, then release.

More recently I was being introduced to the surgeon who would do serious work on my spine. I was very nervous; after we shook hands, he seemed to be examining his to see if it was intact. Now I'm convinced that I have a meaningful, confident handshake. No more cold fish.

The memory of that uncertain time lingers, particularly when I'm about to merge into traffic and my hands become instantly moist.

HOMAGE TO TERESA - THE SUMMER OF 1960

Sometimes, I marvel at how it happens: I read something, or someone mentions a name, or I hear a word in conversation, and I'm instantly transported to another time and place in my life as if a film clip were unreeling on a screen of my mind.

That's what happened when I saw the word "Ligonier," while reading the first few pages of The Johnstown Flood, by David McCullough.

It was in 1960, Woods Hole, Massachusetts. Our little family - husband Gerry, our toddler Ricky, and I - had rented a room in a private house for a week as our summer vacation away from New York City.

We were walking back to our room from having breakfast at a luncheonette. I was wheeling the stroller, Ricky was helping, and Gerry was walking alongside. To my left, on the street, there were one-family houses; to my right, the marina filled with many expensive white boats riding at anchor. A woman was hanging her wash on a line in the yard next door to where we were staying under the watchful eye of a handsome, but very nervous, brown-grey Weimaraner. She called to us in greeting. Surprised at her friendliness we answered in kind; at her invitation, we strolled over to introduce ourselves.

Teresa was of medium height, her blonde hair showed signs of a permanent wave on its way out, she had a lovely smile marred by a missing front tooth that I never noticed again when I heard her incredibly infectious laugh and saw the spirited sparkle in her eyes. We liked each other right away.

She invited us to come over later that evening. When her husband Bill came home from work, the children, four of them came running in to greet him. We met Roddy the oldest, age 12, a lanky boy with straight straw blond hair, intensely blue eyes, and ruddy sun-tanned skin, wearing the summer uniform of shorts, polo shirt, and sandals; Eddy, 10, a smaller, rounder version of his older brother, with a smiling, mischievous glint in his lighter blue eyes; Joy, at 8, already a little mother, a very responsible little girl; and the youngest, Judy, 5, also blonde, but her eyes were dark brown and full of curiosity and mischief.

They were all delightful children; friendly, obedient, relaxed. Judy took to three-year-old Ricky, our little boy right away; they became playmates instantly. The older ones included him in their activities, too. Fritz, the latest to join the group, was a very special dog; he was adopted by the family after having lived in a home where he was seriously abused. High strung, he started at the slightest noise or movement. My heart went out to him, and my fear of dogs, particularly large ones, melted away when I looked into his soulful, beer-colored eyes.

Bill worked as a butler to Retired General Richard Mellon, of the Pittsburgh banking family. He and his wife were spending the summer at their home on Cape Cod. Bill's family was being accommodated nearby in one of the houses along this street.

I had a feeling that this couple was an extraordinary team, and I hoped that when Gerry and I were married for as long as they - I assumed they had been together forever - we would attain as solid a relationship.

It was a wonderful evening. I felt fortunate and grateful to have met such admirable, delightful people. We visited with them again the next day and arranged for a shopping outing to the supermarket and for a picnic in a State Park. At the market, Gerry and I noticed that they were shopping very frugally and that the kids were hungry. We pitched in with cash to defray the cost of the groceries.

One day, they showed us a spectacular private flower garden overlooking the bay that had been opened to the public by a wealthy, civic-minded person. The scent of flowers was evident on the breeze even before we entered. It was the most beautiful suite of gardens in an ideal setting I had ever seen. In addition to a garden filled with an endless variety of roses in every imaginable color, there was an entire walled section filled with blue flowers of many kinds. There were hydrangeas, forget-me-nots, columbines, delphiniums, and irises, to name just a few. Every blossom was exquisite. Every flower bed was perfectly maintained; the place showed good taste, love of flowers, and money, not necessarily in that order.

We had just met, yet we related as if we had known them for years. We enjoyed being in their company and felt a deep kinship with these folks.

On week nights, we met at their house and got better acquainted. Teresa was so much fun. She told anecdotes and laughed at the children's antics and funny sayings. Before our week was over they insisted that we promise to come and stay with them the following summer at their home in Rector, Pennsylvania, where their house was at the entrance of a State Forest. On our part, we assumed that if they invite all three of us to stay for a week they must be able to afford it, and we accepted. At that time, our finances were very low and every penny we spent had to be carefully allocated.

Another day, they drove us out to a lovely spot on a nearby rise overlooking a bay. We picnicked under enormous elm trees, the children had plenty of space to run around and play. Despite the difference in ages, they got along exceptionally well and included our Ricky as if he were one of their siblings. It was a magic day.

The following summer, late evening conversations in the kitchen of the house at the entrance of the State Park revealed brief snippets of Teresa and Bill's story.

They had been married for only six months when we met. Their dramatic underlying back story filled me with sorrow for, as well as awe of this sturdy, amazingly positive woman. During her teens, a local boy took a fancy to her and decided she was to be his. The individual was a bully, and Teresa didn't like him at all. He threatened her family with harm if she didn't comply. Ultimately, she relented and married him. He behaved the way bullies do and kept her in a state of being barefoot and pregnant, as the saying goes. Several pregnancies ended in miscarriages because of his beatings. Eventually, she contrived a way to take herself and her four children beyond the reach of that beastly man; then she worked on becoming legally free.

Bill had been a painter and jack of all trades; he had served in the armed forces. On his return, he found employment as a butler with

General Richard Mellon. Tall, slender, with pale skin, receding straight dark hair, and a slight stoop, he appeared deferential, the quintessential butler, I thought. He was very quiet by nature, but alert, intelligent, extremely polite, and always ready to help. Teresa's and Bill's paths crossed somewhere along the way.

The Mellons liked Bill very much and were supportive of his intention to marry. Bill adopted Teresa's four children, and as they grew, the Mellons paid to send them to the best schools. Later, Bill and Teresa had two more children, to make an even half dozen.

At the end of our week's stay, I had made a close, life-long friend of a woman I met in passing and whose background, education, and religion were poles apart from mine. In 1975, I visited with them in Falmouth, Massachusetts, for a few days in the summer. After that, we kept in touch with occasional letters and pictures for 35 years before she was moved to a nursing home and we lost the connection.

With this torrent of memories still fresh, I had an urge to see if I could locate my friend and find out what she was doing. I went to that magical piece of technology - the internet - where I discovered that she had passed away only a month before. I am very sad that we will never speak to one another again but treasure the time we spent together.

This is the obituary I found:

Komar, Theresa G. 82, Formerly of Ligonier

Theresa G. Komar, 82, formerly of Ligonier, died Wednesday, Oct. 17, 2012, surrounded by her family at Plymouth Crossings where she lived 18 months. Born and raised in Johnstown, she moved to Ligonier in 1960 with her late husband, William B. Komar, to raise their six children. She was a creative, uniquely resourceful and accomplished artist, seamstress and homemaker. She loved her work at a school for disabled children and as a teacher's aide at Ligonier Valley School. She also taught private art lessons. Theresa cherished the summers spent with her family on Cape Cod, and on Bill's retirement, they moved permanently to Sandwich, Mass., to enjoy their children and now grandchildren. She continued painting and creating and also volunteered at the Good Samaritans.

Theresa was survived by her six children, Rod Komar, Ed Komar, Joy O'Keeffe, Judi Knight, Chris Komar and Eric Komar; and 11 grandchildren; a brother, Donald Kordell; and many nieces and nephews. A funeral Mass will be held at 11 a.m. Monday, Nov.12, in St. Joseph's Church in Woods Hole, Mass., followed by a gathering at the Landfall Restaurant in Woods Hole. Burial was private. Memorial donations may be made to the Alzheimer's Foundation at and The Memorial Sloan-Kettering Cancer Center.

IMAGINED EXPECTATIONS - KURT

Early on a recent morning, I was in a parking lot to meet an excursion bus. A car with a man and a woman in it was parking facing my just parked vehicle. I was walking away when the woman called my name in greeting. I turned. I had never seen her before and was puzzled by her friendly tone. She launched into a monologue explaining that she was recruited by a neighbor of mine, a friend of hers, to take her place on the trip. At that point, the young man came out of the car and stood by. The woman kept talking. I didn't know where it all was leading, so I interjected, "So, which of you are coming on the trip today?"

The young man found his voice, "I am. I'm Kurt. Nice to meet you."

The woman continued that he is her cousin and that she was delegating him to take the trip, outlining a plethora of reasons that led to her decision to stay home.

In the seat next to me, Kurt and I settled in for a long ride of 160 miles. For a while, we made small talk regarding the weather, road conditions, and what a comfortable Mercedes bus we were on. Then he said, "I only signed on for this trip because I was promised I could meet you."

"Meet me? Why?"

"I heard about you from my cousin who has your book from her friend, and thought it was a great opportunity."

My sense of responsibility clicked into high gear. What if I don't meet the young man's expectations? What if he's disappointed to find that I'm just a plain, commonplace old lady of no distinction?

This thought triggered a memory that took me back to a day more years ago than I can count; I must have been 18 years old. My mother and I went to visit distant relative Artur Schnabel, a world-class pianist, at his apartment on West 86th Street in New York. I had seen him perform and was appropriately intimidated and awed at the prospect. He was nearly 70, an old man from my perspective at the time. I was a little nervous and excited, expecting him to be somehow larger than life and forbidding in his demeanor.

It came as a surprise when a solid, neatly dressed elderly gentleman with a short crop of thick white hair answered the doorbell and graciously welcomed us like the long-lost relatives we were. He called to his very tall, thin wife to come meet us, and I was delighted to sense that they still adored each other after decades of being together.

In this homey setting, there was something impish about him, something humorous, a spirit that was very different from that which he emanated on stage. During the business of performance, he was an icy perfectionist, making no eye contact with the audience, making no comments, and giving no encores. At those times, only the music was given expression.

At this private encounter, I was unexpectedly at ease and enamored of his personality. He was a charming gentleman, not at all the monolithic presence of the recital stage.

Whatever the young man had heard about me, I hoped that at the end of the day, when we had gone our separate ways, he would be as pleased as I had been after meeting the much-heralded pianist.

IMPRESSION – whose reality is real?

We were still new in town when the mother of one of G's students called to ask that I let her visit and meet with me. Puzzled, I wondered why she would want to do that, but was elated to think someone was interested. We arranged for a Friday afternoon.

She arrived carrying a basket containing a challah and a bottle of Sacramental wine, appropriate house-warming and Sabbath-welcoming gifts for later in the evening. She said the reason for wanting this opportunity was, "Your husband is my daughter's bio teacher, her absolute favorite. I thought he must have a lovely wife, and great children; I *had* to set eyes on and talk to what must be his fabulous family."

Comfortably settled in our living room, we chatted about relocating from the big city with our two boys, changing schools, and many other mundane issues. She often referred to the wonderful life it must be to be the wife of such an outstanding teacher. Her vision or expectation was that we were beautiful to look at, very smart, and always happy. According to her, we must be enveloped by a smiling fortune that made our life flow smoothly and painlessly.

She spoke of my husband's charm, his deep knowledge of the sciences and adolescents; she extolled his patience in explaining new concepts. It was all very gratifying and pleasant for me to hear, but I wished that her glowing descriptions bore some resemblance to my *reality*. At home, the scene for us was fraught with stress. He was perennially dissatisfied with how things were run. Misunderstandings dogged our communications; his desires and standards changing from day to day, there was no satisfying him. The saddest part was that he felt himself to be the only resident in town not blessed with a *decent* family and a good wife.

It was interesting to see how this lady's view of our family differed from *on the ground* reality.

IN DOUBT...?

Look at a kiwi,
a banana,
a pea.
Think of the tides and the moon,
The instincts of creatures to wake and
to mate and to migrate,
each at the appointed time of year.
Accident...?
Happenstance...?
There must be a God.

MEETING THE IBRAGIMOVS

My first day as a bona fide social worker in a New York City agency dedicated to the resettlement of the latest wave of arriving populations from foreign countries began by my being assigned to an experienced supervisor. Mrs. B was a rotund elderly woman, her pink scalp sparsely populated by very short hair dyed ebony. When speaking with her, I could not take my eyes off the patches of skin peeking through the contrasting tufts and thinking how much less noticeable her baldness would be if she used a lighter color.

She was curt and business-like in her manner, and somewhat intimidating to me, only slightly younger than she but a novice in the field. I sat in on her intake sessions to observe and learn her technique; what to ask, how to pace the allotted time of the interview with a client, and what to offer as help. At her behest, I wrote summaries of what transpired during those sessions.

In the fall of 1989, the arrivals were mostly people from the former Republics of the Soviet Union who were immigrating to the United States.

One Monday morning, when I came to her office, she announced, "This morning's intake is yours. You're ready to be on your own."

That unsettled me for a moment, but I reminded myself that I was a "big girl," a midlife career changer, and accepted the first independent assignment in my new profession.

The name on the file she handed me was Ibragimov, the country of origin Uzbekistan. I felt a strange, instant kinship; I lived in that very republic during the war. Memories and images from my past tumbled around in my mind and goose bumps appeared on my forearms.

It was past the appointed hour and there was no sign of them. I remembered that when I was there, Uzbeks didn't have a well-defined grasp of time in the western sense. They functioned on their own system in which *irtaga* was the operative word; it meant later, like the idea of *mañana* in Mexican-Spanish. It worked in that society at that time.

They finally arrived with their two children an hour late. For them, today was also a first experience: negotiating the New York City subway system, which was bewildering and took longer than they had anticipated.

When the formalities of our interview were over, I yielded to the temptation to tell them that I had lived in Uzbekistan during the war. Their curiosity piqued, our instant, and unexpected bond grew closer.

"Where in Uzbekistan did you live?" they wanted to know.

"It was a tiny place with a railroad depot, an oil refinery, and maybe a thousand souls. I'm not sure it's even on the map," I said. "The name of the village was Stancya Vannovskaya."

"Oh, my goodness!!! That's where we are from!" they almost shouted and embraced me. The expression on their faces was one of delight and incredulity. "What a small world!" They told me that the village is now called Hamza in honor of an Uzbek poet of the 19th century.

During the following few months they came to see me several times for follow-up appointments before the agency found them a job and housing in Atlanta, Georgia. That was in 1989. It's 2016; I still think of them and wonder how they're doing.

MEETING SARAH

On a dreary, chilly, January afternoon, my fiancée G and I get off the train at the Pelham Parkway Station in the Bronx, walk three blocks to descend a few stairs into a basement hallway. Halfway down, he rings a door bell. This is it. A loud vociferous barking shatters the quiet of the corridor; I visualize a large, angry dog that will rush at me and tear me apart. My deep-seated, early childhood fear of our four-footed "best friends" overwhelms me; I shrink away in terror of the beast, imagining that when the door opens he'll leap out knock me down and maul me with his sharp teeth and nails.

The reason I am here is that G has asked me to marry him and wants to introduce me to his family. He has told me very favorable things about them.

My palms and toes are damp, my throat is dry, and my breath is quick and shallow. Even my voice is hiding. I wonder if his mother will like me.

"Come on in, it's open," a female voice calls from within. I'm cowering behind G, hoping he'll protect me from the dog. I'm determined not to go through that door. Now I'm sure she won't like me since I'm making a fuss. G listens patiently as I explain how terrified I am. He calls to his mother.

"Put Teddy into your bedroom and latch the gate."

"There's nothing to be afraid of, come on in," she calls back. This is fight or flight. I must decide quickly.

"I'm really sorry, I can't go in unless he's put somewhere. I've always been afraid of dogs, and you didn't tell me you had one," I stammer with as much control as I can muster. I feel trapped and in danger of being bitten by that beast behind the door. I'm ready to abort the mission and have him take me home. Before I consent to step over the threshold, I must be sure the dog is safely in the bedroom and that he won't breach the gate.

As we enter the foyer the barking from the bedroom continues; I can see the big mutt through the doorway trying to leap over the gate, but he can't make it.

G's mother is a slender, youthful-looking woman with a narrow face, black hair, shiny cheekbones, and darting, beady eyes; she looks hardly old enough to be this tall young man's mother. She comes forward to welcome me with what she thinks of as reassuring, "Relax, don't worry, the dog is as lovable as a gentle pussy cat. He won't bite you."

I continue in a state of dread, not sure that's the message I read from the agitated quadruped.

The entry space leads to a living room or, as Sarah calls it, the parlor. A couch upholstered in yellow-green shantung, covered with a thick transparent vinyl slipcover, is against one wall. Two little lamp-topped tables, each one wearing a vinyl shade, flank the couch. On the opposite side of the room there's a TV set in a dark wood cabinet. On a low table between the two lies a neatly folded copy of today's *Daily News*. A fuzzy green wall-to-wall carpet that harmonizes with the rest of the furnishings covers the floor. There's only one picture in the room - on the wall behind the couch, a flattering portrait of a young Sarah done in pastels long ago by an artist in one of the Catskills resorts. Heavy, dark green drapes on the window keep the daylight out. Sarah explains that she replaces them by a lighter floral pattern for the summer.

"Make yourself at home," she says sweetly. I sit down on the slippery plastic that makes a swishy sound against my dress. It feels clammy. Nothing here is out of place. It looks ready for a photo session with *Home Décor* magazine. There isn't a book or periodical in sight. "Does anyone actually live here?" crosses my mind.

The kitchen to the left of the entrance is a deep, narrow space. Three chairs surround a dinette table against the long wall on the right.

"Sit down, dinner's ready," Sarah orders. She serves. We ask her to sit and join us. "I'm not hungry now. Maybe I'll eat later." This is awkward for me; I'm used to all of us having dinner together at home.

During the meal, she keeps urging me to eat more with, "You need to put some meat on your bones," and adding food to my plate without my okay. I don't like it. Soon, she sits down to do official interrogation of the *proposed bride* and asks me questions. I'm sure G has told her that I was born in Europe. During our little chat, it becomes clear that she hears what she fancies, not what I am saying. She is suspicious of me and convinced that I have schemed to marry her son, so I can become an American citizen. She also tells me that she knows that I was reared in a primitive culture in Europe where amenities like telephones and indoor plumbing are unknown. She implies that I discovered them this evening at her home. That mystifies me; it's nowhere near to what I told her about my history. She pointedly shares with me the fact that her mother's house was so clean, "You could eat off the floor." As I picture them eating off the floor, I wonder why one would want to, since here in the West we have used tables and chairs for many centuries.

George, the paterfamilias, is a man of sturdy build with a deeply tanned face and electric blue eyes. When he comes home from work, his booming voice sounds as if he's shouting all the time. G explains that he works in a fruit market at a very busy intersection in the Bronx and is used to making himself heard at that decibel level. He washes up and sits down to eat in the chair that Sarah has just vacated.

After a few bites of dinner, it's his turn to interrogate me. It's a grilling. "What do you do? Where do you work?"

I tell him that I'm between jobs and going to school. He seizes on that.

"Between jobs? A rolling stone… Oh! You go to college?" In an audible aside to his son, he says: "She goes to college; you know what college girls are, don't you? They're sluts." He sounds as if he, too, is convinced that he's imparting Absolute Truth. I'm young, inexperienced, and polite; I am not prepared to be insulted and don't know how to parry this approach. I sit still wishing this wasn't happening.

Eventually, G and I signal each other that it's time to leave. In preparation for the last move, Sarah, G, and I are standing close together in the foyer saying our good-byes and thank-yous for dinner. She steps back, looks me over appraisingly, and forecasts the future, "You'll never have children; you have no hips."

We say our good-byes; I mutter the obligatory, "Nice to meet you."

Teddy barks often enough to keep me aware of his presence, but less wildly than earlier. He, too, is tired. I'm glad to have this evening behind me and sense that it's going to be a rough ride through married life.

MURPHY'S LAW IS ALIVE AND WELL

Soon after my husband and I moved to San Diego, I read about a call for artists to submit work for a projected exhibition to honor veterans. I remembered I had two interesting photographs appropriate to the subject and decided to submit them. Happily, I located them easily despite the uprooting of my household. Great start! Upon examining them thoroughly to make sure the presentation was intact, I saw the mat on one was slightly damaged. A new mat is no problem, but where did I put them? I looked for the carton in which I thought they were, but it was marked "Drawing and watercolor papers."

A search through every closet and portfolio in our apartment began. I agonized a while, tried to visualize their location, scolded myself about my lack of accurate memory, and eventually returned to the original box. This time, when I opened it the mats were there clean and ready to be used as expected. Now I could get on with it! Just have to remove the frame, change the mat, and put the whole thing back together. I can do that in a trice.

Things aren't always as they seem. The old mat was wedged tightly to the frame and I had to pry it out, doing more damage to it. That didn't matter. I changed the mat for a new one, returned the picture in the frame, and placed a backing on it. Now I needed to use the Frame Master to secure the glazier points to lock the whole thing up. That's easy. The box was in the closet where I thought, but the glazier points weren't in it. I made another tour of the closets, did more visualizing, more searching. When I finally found them, and had the Frame Master ready to work, the wood proved too hard and they bounced off instead of penetrating into it to hold the frame to the rest of the contents. Now what? I had another frame of the same size. I switched the glass pane to the new frame, but it didn't fit by a fraction of a centimeter. You would think glass from frames of the same size would be interchangeable. Not so in this case. By now I was getting frustrated and tired. Do I really want to submit to this show?! Of course, I do!

Counting to ten slowly, while taking a deep breath to bolster my resolve, I searched for and found another frame with glass. Starting over I got the job finished. The mat fits the frame and the backing, the glazier points are in, the eye hooks in their places, and the label is made.

The work is ready to hang on a wall.

MY NEW WORLD

I marked my 12th birthday while crossing the Atlantic, lying on my bunk, deathly seasick. A few days later, on March 24, 1947, the *Drottningholm* docked in the Port of New York during a severe early spring rainstorm. The expectation of solid ground beneath my feet gave me scant comfort. I was too anxious, not having any notion of what was awaiting. The rain was heavy and continuous.

******

My mother and I were on a long queue of arrivals waiting to be processed at the line of tables set up for the purpose in the narrow corridor on the way out of the ship. We were more than ready to disembark after a particularly turbulent crossing of the Atlantic from Goteborg, Sweden. The functionaries scrutinized everyone's documents and asked questions. One stands out in my memory for its sheer absurdity.

"Are you coming to the United States with the purpose of killing the President?" the official asked my shy, unassuming, and anxious mother, as if it was a perfectly normal thing to do. Even then, and with her limited knowledge of English, she noticed the inanity. This was no time for making jokes.

We were glad to be on terra firma, at the goal we had hoped for these several years. At first, we were moving along with the pace of the crowd, slowly, seeing nothing but the backs of the people ahead of us in the semi-darkness of the narrow passage. Then the view widened as we came closer to the edge of the deck. The eyes of the arriving passengers were searching the faces in the throng waiting at the pier for their relatives to identify the one important one; to heave the sigh of relief at being found, smile and wave in recognition from afar before embracing in greeting after descending the gangplank.

My mother had told me that my Uncle Fred would be there to greet us. I watched for her eyes to light up and her lips break into a smile at any moment. It didn't happen. Her brow furrowed ever tighter and my fear of *the new* rose ever higher. What would happen to us in this miserable, cold, wet place if no one came? Suppose my uncle forgot?

Suddenly, we heard "Gretl! Gretl!"

My mother turned; there was a black-clad, barrel-like form on two skinny legs, wearing a black hat with a stylish veil screening her face, waving her hand energetically, coming toward us. When she made her way through several layers of people and reached us, she introduced herself to my mother.

"I'm Aunt Frieda, Artur Schnabel's sister. You remember him, don't you? I'm here to fetch you because Fred couldn't make it. I am going to take you to your Cousin Lola's home for the night and then we'll see what you need to do. Follow me." She was all business.

She turned, and we followed her out to the crowded, wet, noisy, gun-metal gray street in front of Manhattan's Pier 57. I wondered what my mother was thinking. As for me, I just wanted to be away from the ship and the tumult, the cold and the rain. My fantasy of being welcomed with open arms on a sunny day materialized into a different reality, frankly grim.

Out in the street, there was a steady stream of several rows of cars going in the same direction. Many were bright yellow with several numbers and the words "Yellow Cab," or had a checkerboard pattern and the word "Checker" printed on the door. Each car had a light on top of its roof. When it was on, the taxi was available for hire. We walked to the edge of the pavement.

Aunt Frieda said, "Wait here," and raised her arm to signal.

One of these yellow cars pulled close, stopped, and the driver stepped out. He ushered us into the back seat, then he opened a compartment in the rear of the car and loaded the suitcases in it, got behind the wheel, and asked, "Where-to, Ma'am?" Aunt Frieda gave him an address and we pulled from the curb to merge into the stream of traffic.

It was wonderful to be away from the chill and looking out the taxi window as we rode in private luxury through rain-soaked streets crowded with vehicles and people rushing this way and that. I noticed that some of the passersby had very dark skin and, for the most part, wide noses. I asked my mother about them and she explained they were people with ancestry in Africa and were called Negroes, as *negro* is the word for black in Spanish and Italian. That made sense and I thought no more about it. It was the first time I saw what was then called a Negro. Over time, the politically correct word to refer to this group of people morphed to Colored, then to Black, and currently, in the 21st century, it's African-American.

After making some turns to the left and some to the right we stopped in front of a very tall building. The driver opened our door, lifted the baggage out of the trunk, and my aunt paid him. A uniformed doorman wearing impressively clean white gloves hurried to usher us into the building with a wide welcoming sweep of his arm. Inside, the lobby was large and very dignified. Subdued lighting and large mirrors behind oversize bouquets of fresh flowers reflected the elegant space making a big impression on me. Thickly carpeted floors silenced what sound our footsteps might have made. Pictures of landscapes hung on the walls, each with its own light above it. The setting was beautiful, strange, and spooky. The uniformed man escorted my aunt, mother, and me into an elevator that also had mirrors on its walls. The operator was dressed like the doorman, gloves and all.

My aunt said, "Twenty-nine, please."

In the time it took to say, "Yes Ma'am," we were there. I felt as if I had left my stomach behind downstairs. We stepped out on a landing where there was only one door and, again, carpeting, a mirror, and a huge bouquet of fresh flowers.

Aunt Frieda rang the bell. A dark faced woman opened the door a crack. She said that the lady of the house was out and left no instructions to let anyone with suitcases in. The fear of being stuck with nowhere to go made my heart beat faster and the nausea still left over from the voyage increased. I pictured having to go back to the street and being stranded. My aunt explained who we were; the dark woman told us that she was the housekeeper and her name was Rose. Reluctantly, she let us in, with the caveat that we would stay in the study to await Lola's return. Only then would we know what awaited us.

Things took a more favorable turn later in the day when Lola's explanation for what happened was that she had forgotten to let Rose know of our expected arrival. It had to be sufficient. She invited us to make ourselves comfortable and Rose brought tea and cookies. The good news of the day was that my mother and I would stay with the cousin's family for two weeks until my father's arrival on the Swedish ship *Gripsholm*, at which time we would have to make other arrangements.

MY TIME FOR PRAYER

"You have a 20% chance of losing the use of your arms. That nerve that I have to push aside doesn't like to be disturbed."

"Twenty percent?" I gasped, trying to wrap my mind around exactly what those words meant, and projecting my life going forward, possibly without being able to do self-care things like brush my teeth, dress, or feed myself, and myriad things, way too many to mention, that I've done for 65 years of my life.

We were discussing the forthcoming procedure to remove two ruptured disks that were pressing into my spinal cord and to replace the space with synthetic bone and fuse the whole thing. The assistant must have sensed my horror, because she said quietly, "This is elective surgery, you can change your mind and decide not to come in that morning."

I could not conceive living in the grip of continuing, unrelieved pain in my shoulders, neck, and arms, nor could I imagine being so totally disabled. Neither option was attractive. I wondered, what were the odds that I would lose the gamble? Aloud, I asked, "What if I don't do it?"

"Your arms will get weaker and additional disks may rupture from the strain put on them." With that the slightly built, athletic figure of the surgeon turned his back on me and disappeared through the door, leaving me in a heap of unresolved doubt and fear.

I didn't know which way to decide. My condition was affecting not only my life, but also my husband's, and if things became worse and I became helpless, how would that play out? A thousand scrambled, unhappy scenarios dashed through my unsettled brain.

We had moved across the country, hoping the mild climate would be a new beginning for the senior years. Was this what it would look like?

I would have to go through with it. At least there was a chance that I would win.

"Now remember, if you choose not to go through with it, just don't come in," the assistant repeated reassuringly. Easy for her to say.

My husband held my hand, and after the medical personnel had left, he said, "It's completely your choice, darling. I'll do whatever you decide."

At that moment, deep down, I really wished someone else would make that decision.

On S-day, the morning of the surgery, I tried, as usual, to be humorous under severe stress. I was flat on my back when an orderly named Ramon came to hook up an IV in my arm. I greeted him with a smile. After three tries he told me I had bad veins and, after the fourth try, he got up, left a needle stuck half-way in my arm, and stormed out in anger, saying "You have lousy veins! I can't do this!" By then I was so upset that I made it my business to remember his name. A female came in, calmly finished finding my vein, and I was wheeled, half-awake, into the operating theater.

At this point, aware of my utter impotence and lack of control, I found myself thinking, "Dear God, please inspire the surgeon's hands and mind to get me through this with my brain undamaged by anesthesia and my arms intact." Then the anesthesia took hold and I lost consciousness.

When I came to, there was a nurse saying something quietly, something like, "How do you feel? You'll be ready to go to your room in a little while."

As I awakened, I remembered the threat that loomed a short time ago. I realized that I had been actively moved to prayer for the first time in my life. My arms were still there at my sides. I tried to wiggle my fingers. I could. Then I tried to raise the arms one at a time, I did. My body was intact.

The orderly wheeled me into a corridor where my husband was waiting. I was so overcome with joy that tears flooded my eyes and I couldn't speak. I raised both my arms, signaled for him to bend toward me, and hugged him to show they were all right and doing what they were meant to do.

NEW TIRES - A CHALLENGE

My husband always took care of auto related issues. Now, I must deal with these things on my own. Ever since the mechanic told me I needed a set of new tires, I have been mulling about when, where, and how to decide on what kind of tires to buy. As time went by, the notion became an anxiety-laden project. Friends suggested I "shop around for the best price"; others said, "Make sure you get good value for your money." Over dinner, one gave me the best suggestion: "See what's on the car now and get the same, only with new treads. Done. No big deal." That sounded like a plan to me.

It rained that week and I avoided driving. That was enough time for the task to grow huge in my mind. On the day the rain stopped, I set myself the goal to have brand new tires installed on my very old car.

In a reasonably high state of anxiety, I drove to the nearest link in a chain of stores my mechanic suggested. A neatly uniformed, tall, slender young man with a bright smile was coming toward me as I stepped out of my car in the parking lot.

"How can I help you?" he asked in a voice that melted all my uneasiness away. I felt that I was in good hands. I told him what I needed, gave him my keys, and we went inside the facility. He took my information, wrote it down, offered me some water, and ushered me to a seat. I felt relaxed and comfortable. That was easy.

After what seemed like a long time another young man came in and called my name. "Here I am!" I jumped up confident that all was ready for me to drive away.

"Where's the lug nut key?" he asked. Uh oh!

I know it's a very important, albeit small piece of equipment, and remembered that I recently put it where it would always be at hand. "Think fast!" I told myself as my heart raced; my hands became damp and my mouth dry. Without that tool, the wheels can't be removed, and the tires can't be replaced. "Look in the plastic bag where the manual is on the back seat," I said, trying to sound much more efficient than I felt.

"It's not there," he reported back just as confidently.

"Okay, try the pocket in the driver's side door."

"Not there either."

"How about the console between the front seats?" I ventured as a creeping desperation took hold of my thinking and I had nowhere else to turn for an idea. "Where can I get one?"

"Well, you can go to a VW dealer. They can probably supply one," the young man replied in a "problem solved" voice. To me that was the worst news I could hear.

"Where is one?" I asked, just to keep the communication open.

"I really don't know, but there must be one in San Diego," he answered casually.

Ashamed of my cowardice, I confessed, "I don't drive freeways."

I sensed the little independence of coming and going on my own I have left coming to a screeching halt. In a last gesture of hope, I went out to the car and put my hand into the center console. My fingers touched something metal and I pulled it out. The lug nut key!!! Halleluiah!

Eventually, the first young man came back, the tires were on, and I was ready to go. I paid him and, with the proverbial song in my heart, I set off for home on my brand-new tires, happy to have met, and overcome, yet another challenge of the independence that widowhood imposes.

OBSERVATIONS ON SHOPPING - Barbara O.

I notice that some women pride themselves on owning expensive silverware, china, crystal, linens, and other assorted furnishings in their homes. They sometimes go to great lengths to acquire objects like unique hand painted cups and saucers of fine china to place on display in what is called the hutch, usually in a corner in the dining room. For some, redecorating is an ongoing lifetime process. No sooner have they replaced most of the objects in the home than they start over in their desire to update, to change, and to keep up with the rapidly changing latest fashion. They are unendingly changing slip covers, selecting new color schemes, making decisions, buying, waiting for delivery, hanging new drapes. Then there's the returning of slightly or seriously damaged goods or wrong colors to stores. All this provides a cycle of intense activity month after month and year after year, sometimes until the lady of the house becomes too disabled by age or illness to continue.

Recently, on an errand to a store, I met a neighbor who seems to be a busy lady. She was on her way to the check-out counter pushing a cart filled with an assortment of items. Seeing me, she called me over.

"Look at these! Aren't they lovely?" she asked triumphantly, holding up two huge coffee mugs with roses painted on them. She turned them around fully to be sure I got the full impact of their beauty from all sides. Then she brought tapered candles, an area rug, and a few other items out of her shopping cart.

"I'm here at least twice a week," she added. I know that this lady lives by herself and has a fully equipped apartment with enough dishes to feed a scout troop and their parents.

"What will you use these things for?" I asked, puzzled why she would come as often as she said she does.

"Oh, I could have hot chocolate or tea in them," she answered with a happy lilt in her voice.

We said our adieus and I continued the mission that had brought me to the store.

I remembered encountering the same neighbor, her eyes sparkling with happiness, returning from a bargain-shopping expedition, her cart laden with household "goodies" a month before. Now and then, I see a large pile of things wrapped in plastic trash bags waiting to be carted off to a resale shop at her apartment door. It seems to me this lady likes shopping as a sport.

I began to think about a possible reason why it is that I put so little store by the acquisition of items and don't feel deep pride in ownership when I do buy something. If I need something, I go to a store. If I find it, it's attractive, the price is right, I buy it; done.

I never owned any significant silver, crystal, or china pieces, or had a trousseau with fancy monogrammed linens like other girls. The purchases of furnishing for our apartment when I got married were preferably modular, so when the circumstances changed they could be used in different configurations. I was concerned with paying the rent and making the place comfortable and attractive. Perhaps it comes from a deep-seated sense of instability with the potential need to move at a moment's notice, and the need to travel light, that war conditions taught me as a very young child. I have always lived in places, no matter how primitive, made attractive by my mother and haven't given the matter any thought regarding the reason for my lack of acquisitiveness ever since.

Now, I find that I prefer to spend my time and energy making things. I take delight in the process of creating something, be it a design, a piece of written work, or a sculpture from found objects I collected.

I don't recommend this approach to others but find that acceptance of my impermanence suits me. To quote a very old French adage: *"Chacun a son gout"* or "To each his own."

ON LOSS - ABOUT MY MOTHER - October 28, 2002

Yesterday, Dr. Pisano, from New Rochelle Hospital, called to tell me that mother passed away at 1:45 AM, Saturday, October 27, reportedly in her sleep. He said he signed the death certificate at that time.

Today, I'm not sure just what I'm feeling; an undifferentiated mixture of sadness, grief, pity, and relief, all coming together in a strange numbness. There won't be any more memories to add to the strands that made the rich tapestry of our mutual unconditional love and respect for one another during our long relationship. That tapestry is finished, whether I like it or not.

We had been through a lot from a relatively plush beginning, through a war with its privations and uncertainties, luckily ending in the land of promise – the United States of America. I realize that a major part of my own life is also over as I am a senior citizen myself. For the first time, my mom isn't there for me to talk things over. I could never imagine what it would be like not to have her somewhere within voice-reach. Now, I must truly grow up.

In a way, I feel relieved that her misery won't continue any longer. At the practical level, I have mourned my mother for the last six years, since the geriatric psychiatrist told me that she was beyond a point from which the person I knew could be reclaimed. That day, he told me, "It's time for you to grow up and live your life."

It took me some time to relinquish the hope I had that we could reverse the gradual process of losing her to her demons and depression. Her quick mind, wide range of interests, curiosity about the world, nimble fingers that made beautiful things, from dresses to sweaters to paintings to sculptures, were a thing of the past. Her usually sincere conviction that she was doing her best in the moment no matter how challenging the situation was replaced by someone indifferent, dissatisfied, in the grip of unrelieved moroseness.

Since July 17, 2002, when Mother sustained yet another of a series of falls, she has not recovered. This time it was a hip fracture. She was brought back from the hospital after the surgery with a wound on her back which would not heal. She could no longer be placed in a wheel chair, only turned in bed. She has spent most of the days sleeping, unresponsive, refusing medication as well as nourishment. This was certainly not a life of quality; it was not anywhere near what she would have found acceptable.

Powerless to help, I have been suffering with her. I felt upset with the care or lack of it that she was receiving in the nursing home. Even before this last incident, I was frustrated to see her loss of self-determination, loss of control of body and mind, and above all I felt deep sorrow for her expression of total dissatisfaction with everything. That was the worst. There was nothing I could say or do for her, nothing I could give her, nowhere I could take her that made any difference. The deep depression that gripped her reached its tentacles toward me.

It seems that Mother had either not realized years ago or simply not accepted that the aging process would claim her just as it does everyone, and she had not made internal arrangements to deal with the decreasing abilities that she would have to deal with. She might have felt outside the mainstream of humanity in that respect. She was a very private person, a soul apart; always friendly, yet a loner, with great intelligence, charm, and spirit. As beloved as she was by the people around her, it seems she rarely if ever gave of herself to them.

It hurt me deeply to see my mother not accepting her present reduced self, and to be so impotent to help. No amount of entertaining, visiting, or goodies, could draw her out of the black mood.

Years have passed. When I came across the draft of this piece, my thoughts surrounding the deaths of other loved ones, and related experiences surfaced.

I have a theory that the lack of proper nutrition affected the quality of my mother's mental functioning. A person who didn't like food, and ate only to sustain life, she was never hungry, often forgot to have a meal, and when reminded would eat a small piece of dry bread and drink a cup of coffee. That pattern began to be serious in the early nineteen nineties. I believe dehydration and starvation were the primary causes of her dementia setting in at that time, and that appropriate consumption of nutrients would have staved off the onset for a while longer. The osteoporosis was already well established, but even that could have probably been slowed with better nutrition, had she been less stubborn.

Now she's gone. Just like that, a person turned into a "body."

It occurs to me that perhaps when a person feels no longer willing to continue life, the ability for intake of food lessens and acts as a mechanism to help one die. I also wonder how people say good-bye, if they do. I'm not sure that I have.

In my first encounter with this type of loss, my husband Gerry died unexpectedly; however, I had mourned our relationship for several years before the fact of his unexpected physical death, because he isolated himself from me. When he died, the void he left was probably different from what it would have been had we had a steady flow of communication.

My father was ailing, but also died unexpectedly. He, like my mother, couldn't accept his reduced condition and became a very unhappy person; a changed man after a mild stroke. He fell into depression and withdrew. I knew that at his age there was only one direction, but always hoped his spirits would pick up and he would enjoy what he had. His path was a distancing that lasted for ten years, and then one afternoon it stopped.

In mother's case, it was similar; during the last five years of her life she focused inward on her own confusion and resulting feelings of worthlessness, rejecting attempts to nourish, entertain, or cheer. She became ever less responsive, sleeping more and more, until her heart stopped. It was deeply sad.

All this brings me to recognize that we who are left behind are made resilient to live beyond and to absorb our inevitable losses and that each grief is unique within its universality.

ONE MORNING IN LWOW/LVIV/LEMBERG

In late fall of 1939, I was four-years-old. The extended family on my mother's side had gathered in Lwow, a city on the edge of eastern Poland, at the apartment belonging to my grandfather's sister, Aunt Tina. We were there to outrun Hitler's invasion of Poland that began on September 1. We accepted her hospitality in hopes of saving ourselves from his deadly intentions.

Both my parents, two grandparents, and an assortment of their siblings met under that roof hoping for safety and to retain a modicum of sanity by being together. I listened to conversations and discussions about the events of the day before; who hid where overnight, who was missing, and assumed to have been taken away, what were the Soviets going to do now that the Germans retreated? Plans were made to go to the town square to listen and to look and to meet again later.

One early morning, when we were getting ready for breakfast, an insistent banging and loud voices at the door sent a wave of fear and anxiety through us all. A bunch of shouting, soldiers stormed into the apartment pointing rifles with bayonets at us. Yelling at us in Russian and shoving us roughly out of their way they ransacked each room, pulled out drawers, tossed the clothes around, all the while angrily shouting something none of us understood. They were getting angrier and louder as they seemed to be searching for something and wanted to know where it is. All we could do is be terrified into silence and helplessness. Who were these awful beastly beings? I wondered. What did they want? What was their rage all about? None of us could answer them.

After a few minutes that felt much longer, they gestured for all except Aunt Tina to make a bundle of bedding, clothes, and personal articles. They showed us on the clock that we had 30 minutes to get downstairs. As a permanent resident of the city, she was ordered to stay in her home.

In the rush and the chaos no one could think, and we did as we were ordered. Downstairs, a truck with many frightened people already on it was waiting to add us to its load. The soldiers indicated that there was to be no talking among us, as were now considered "enemies of the people."

And so, it was that we were brought to the Lwow railroad station that morning. We were not alone; trucks with similar cargo of stunned terrified people were arriving in a steady stream. Long trains of box cars were waiting to receive us. We were crowded into them by the truckload and locked from the outside. By evening, we began our journey to the unknown.

*****

Note: 1. Aunt Tina was left behind, alone in her large apartment, because only refugees were being taken. No further information regarding her life or death has ever become known. We don't know where, when, or how she met her dreadful fate.

2. Lwow is a city founded in the 13th century. It was considered culturally important and was to be defended from the Nazis at all costs. It was heavily bombed in September 1939, when Germany invaded Poland. The Soviet invasion of Poland was intended to be a saving gesture to prevent Hitler from getting too close.

RANDOM BEGINNING

At times, I feel overwhelmed by all the thoughts of things I want to or need to do that have taken up residence in my brain simultaneously. I find myself starting to sort the old papers, but "no, this will take too long… some other time." Then I finger the pile of months-old magazines… they'll take a long time to go through. Oh, yes, and those pictures from the trip before last that need printing and arranging into an album… The letter I need to write to a friend needs some thought, so I'll do that at another time…

I wander from task to task, pausing just long enough at each place to increase my level of frustration and confusion, until my eye falls on a task such as the unmade bed, or the clothes from the night before that need hanging up. That takes only a moment to do, but provides me with the catalyst, even if it is random, I seem to require organizing the chaos in my mind to begin reasonable orderly positive action.

REFLECTION ON THE PAST

Reflecting on the past, especially the knotty, difficult times, I see with the clarity of hindsight, instances when I should have followed my heart and taken a firm stand. Instead, I acted weakly or failed to act at all, out of fear of being left alone with two children. I didn't have what I thought were marketable skills to make a living to support them, and there was nothing to fall back on. I imagined myself on the street with them. In that dire, fatalistic frame of mind, I let the situation take me where it would.

Sometimes, I wonder what would have happened had I fought back, refused to take the one-down position even once. What turn would my children's lives have taken had I left early on, when I realized that we were in a no-win situation?

The reality is, I didn't take any of those proactive and risky steps. The enormity of uncertainty immobilized me. That way I didn't expose myself. All that's left is idle and wasteful fantasies of what might have been.

ROADSIDE SHRINE

A memorial shrine, a cross entwined with colorful plastic flowers, and the name "Tony" stenciled on a crossbar was recently erected on a road I travel daily. A young driver died here. Racing.

There are many shrines around. Such displays usually commemorate the place where a fatality on wheels took place, and some the site of a murder. In most cases, it's the location where the violence took place that becomes transformed into a decorative memorial space filled with flowers, cards, and pictures in appreciation of the deceased. Sometimes, more permanent stone or granite memorials are erected.

When Princess Diana died, the people showed their mass grief by creating a space for the deposit of tributes near her home. Thousands brought their flowers and trinkets to add to the already extensive display. It seems to be a custom, dating back hundreds of centuries, as seen in ancient plaques at sites where births, deaths, and battles have taken place.

As I often pass this shrine. It makes me wonder what deep psychic need we humans have that is served by this type of display. What type of comfort does it provide to frame out a space along the road and decorate it to make passersby aware of someone's grief? Is it a sorrowful warning or shared grief, or joy in the case of a victory in battle? A curious, universal custom.

RUMINATION ON SHOES AND TOES

From the time when man first walked the earth, feet needed protection from injury and cold. Today footwear is made of many materials and colors, in styles appropriate to various types of activity such as heavy industry, business, recreation, or to accommodate unusual conditions of working in water, on ice, or in outer space. In all of those places, the toes are fully covered.

Making my way through security checks and hurrying along with the crowd at airports, I became aware that I was in the minority of people, especially females wearing what I define as real shoes. By that I mean shoes that cover the entire foot including the toes. For clarity's sake, let me say that I use the word "bare" to refer to the feet of people wearing footwear constructed of a sole and a variety of arrangements of straps to hold the foot in place. The top of the foot is exposed.

I have noticed for several years that thongs, also called flip-flops, and strips of various widths, attached to soles ranging from cheap quarter-inch thick plastic with a strap that is placed between the first two toes purchased in a dime store, to high priced platform soles and high-fashion decorated straps that cost a king's ransom, have replaced the shoe and have been in vogue for several years. As I started to take a good look at feet, I noticed that their characteristics are as unique as those of other parts of our anatomy; that there are an infinite number of malformations, and that the shape of a person's feet is hereditary in many details.

Usually, homo sapiens have five toes on each foot in a standard arrangement from the largest diminishing in size toward the smallest. On some feet, all five toes are nearly the same length, others have a subtly graduated difference in size between the first and last toe. Some feet are wide; some are so narrow that they are almost reminiscent of fins. The array is endless; add to that the variations of deformities caused by too short, tight, or narrow shoes in early life, and the mix is even greater. There are toes that grew over one another like crossed fingers, perhaps from shoes that were too tight, and others have a bony growth over the knuckles, from having worn styles that were too short.

Some toes seem to be non-conformists and have taken their own direction or curled back on themselves. The deformities that were previously hidden by a shoe are now on proud display. In fact, they are decorated to attract attention. Painted toe nails in as enormous a range of colors as the selection of samples in a house-paint store and paste-on patterns ranging from floral to geometric are on feet everywhere.

The bare feet have become a feature that draws the eye, a definite fashion statement; far afield from the need to protect from the elements - the basic reason foot covering originated.

The podiatry, pedicure, and massage business in general must be booming as never before, considering the millions of "bare" feet walking in crowded places where everyone is in a hurry and the risk of having toes stepped on or falling headlong because someone else stepped on one's sole is very high. In airports, stairs, on unpaved trails, and industrial spaces especially, there's the risk of stubbing or breaking the toes, or having something heavy dropped on them.

Is this a manifestation of the decadence of our society?

THE ADVENUTRE OF FRAMING

This is one of those "if it can go wrong, it will," events that are hilarious in a silly sort of way.

A friend was about to celebrate a significant birthday. After thinking long and hard about what I could do to make him smile, I remembered two charming photos of one of his great grandchildren and hit on the idea of matting and framing them as a gift. So far, so good. I printed them next to each other on one page, bought an appropriate frame, and cut a mat. Everything was set; I assembled the elements, took an appraising look, and felt satisfied that he would enjoy receiving it. I wrapped it in gift paper, attached a card, and put it away to await the day of celebration.

The following day, about to set up my desk for painting, I noticed a large piece of glass lying in my way. It dawned on me that I had forgotten to replace it in the frame. Uh oh! Simple, I thought. Take the wrapper off, insert the glass, we're in business.

If that were so, I wouldn't be telling this story.

When I opened the package, there was a smudge of glue on the edge of the mat causing an unsightly mark. I tried to clean it away with a special soft eraser. The rubbing roughed up a strip of the photo paper making it worse. I had no more material to cut a mat to a new size, so I thought I would reprint the picture. Things in my computer being what they are, I couldn't find it and most of the day went by while I dealt with all sorts of connected side steps before I did. When I re-printed it, it wasn't as well centered as I wanted. I checked and looked and measured, but it wasn't just right. Back I went to the proverbial square one or the drawing board. Finally, I decided on an expedient way to put it all back together, fixed it, rewrapped it, and it was ready for presentation.

THE DAY OF THE WEDDING

In 1989, November 22 was the day before Thanksgiving. Despite it being the anniversary of the assassination of JFK and the sad memories that evoked, Robert and I made plans to get married.

Our agenda that day was to move his possessions from his house to mine in the morning before the formal ceremony in the afternoon. In a nod to the tradition of not seeing the bride before the big event, he spent the night in his house.

When I awoke that morning, my usually wavy, manageable hair was a mass of dark gray sticks poking out in every direction from my scalp; it didn't respond to a comb in its usual cooperative way.

"Oh well," I thought. "Later, when I wet it, it will."

There were other, more immediate things to attend to. My dressers needed to be emptied and moved out of the bedroom to make room for his, and spaces had to be re-configured to accommodate two people where, for 14 years, there had been only one.

When I fretted about all this, Bob reassured me. "We'll do it; don't worry. I have an idea how."

First, to make room, we moved my dressers down the narrow staircase to the basement. Then at his house, we carried his down the stairs and loaded them into the Bronco for the two-mile ride to their new home. We maneuvered the heavy, bulky pieces of furniture around a corner and down the even narrower stairs of his house and up an equally tight space to the bedroom in mine.

Moving furniture with Bob was like participating in a well-choreographed dance. Evidently, he had thought out and planned every step, because he directed me verbally and we carried out the move without a hitch. We worked together amazingly well. With his masterful instructions, we accomplished the transfer without a scratch or a nick on any of the pieces, and in record time. We must have been so psyched that we weren't even tired.

Thinking back on that sun-less, windy, emotionally charged morning, I don't know how we did it so smoothly and well without a cross word between us. The only issue was my suddenly straight unruly hair. While working with Bob an idea came to me. I went to the florist, bought a length of pink ribbon and some baby's breath. I put the two together into a decorative headband. Problem solved. It looked very pretty.

I was waiting for a case of jitters to set in; it didn't. All was well. By three o'clock we were in the Temple sanctuary greeting our guests.

The Rabbi, looking like God's younger brother with his white beard and black robes stepped under the *(huppah)* wedding canopy with us. He gave a talk emphasizing the power of words. Having been at the receiving end of some harsh pronouncements in the past, it resonated with me at a deep level. Words can be kind and nurturing or profoundly wounding; once uttered they cannot be taken back or nullified but are likely to imbed themselves into the soul.

He ended with, "Always think before you speak."

A good precept to practice in life.

THE DENTAL APPOINTMENT

I'm in the dentist's chair with a bib secured around my neck, waiting for the chief tooth fairy to come in to check the job the tech did in cleaning my ivories, and to share information regarding my options with respect to the question I had asked about the appearance of a small, darkened but still serviceable baby tooth; by some miracle it's still strong and in place after over seventy years of use.

Stepping energetically, the dentist strides in, her bright eyes shining, her lips parted in a welcoming smile. In her hand, there's what looks like a key ring. This one has little wire spokes that end in tiny tiles; the little off-white squares make a clear, pretty, chime-like sound when they clink gently against one another. "This is the scale of tooth colors" she explains, "and by that measure your teeth are the darkest."

Where's all this going? I wonder. *I only asked about a possible crown; if it can be done, and what it would cost.*

She's not listening to me; she's on a roll, detailing a process.

"Your teeth could be bleached in the office in an hour or if you prefer, you can do it yourself by sleeping with a device that holds the bleaching agent in your mouth over a year of nights."

All that is very interesting, but it doesn't address my question.

She continues, "Your incisors are in a congenitally switched position, and your smile will be prettier when the teeth are crowned and white, so you have to decide before we have them fabricated. The porcelain crowns can't be tinted after they're installed."

So, when do we talk about what I want to know? I wonder silently. I realize that I must do something to stop this super cheery sales talk; I don't intend to buy today; in fact, most likely not ever.

"What about the long-term effects on my mouth chemistry?" I finally interrupt, to slow down the momentum of the sales pitch, and take advantage of the moment to say, "So far my teeth have been through a lot. They have withstood a war with early-life nutritional privations, as well as lack of basic sanitation at that time. Why would I take a chance on weakening them now? Anyway, I'm pleased to have my own teeth at this advanced age."

The dentist tells me that the process has been in use for ten years, there's nothing to worry about, and, "It's possible that chemical change may improve the flora in your mouth. Isn't being more attractive important?" *I keep my own counsel.*

A memory of a scene in "On Golden Pond," an old movie, occurs to me. In it, an elderly couple (Katherine Hepburn and Henry Fonda) are opening their summer cottage. There's a picture from their youth on the mantelpiece; he looks at it, squints, and says, "Who the hell is that?"

I tell my dentist that after all these years of being very self-critical, I finally accept my appearance and that if she were to change it, I would look in the mirror and most likely be tempted to quote Henry Fonda by saying, "Who the hell is that?" to the reflection.

THE DISORDER OF MEMORIES

It's close to midnight; I'm brushing my teeth, the final act of the day before getting into bed for the rest I need to have a reasonably productive next day.

Unbidden, random thoughts apropos to nothing that I'm aware of, wisps of memories of events decades ago or yesterday, dance, sometimes gallop or clomp heavily across the "mind place" where I imagine the screen for remembering must be located. Sometimes it's like a continuous film strip showing events of the past strung together in a haphazard sequence of unrelated events with no chronology. I don't know how or why it happens but assume it's a universal phenomenon. Maybe it's just that I noticed.

So, at this late hour, while carrying out the most mundane of activities, it comes to me, out of context now, that I met Bob socially for the first time when I was 46, at a get-together for single people. We married when I was 54. Irrelevant? Out of context? Totally.

In the mental images immediately following that wisp of memory, I'm in my late twenties on a beach at the edge of Lake Champlain with my children. What's the connection? Nothing I can fathom. Why would that cross my mind at this moment? Other mental images follow: the intervening years, snippets of major life-changing trials and half-forgotten happenings that are all part of the string of days, months, and years coalescing into some sort of background "Gestalt."

The realities of life for me were involved in meeting the needs of work, my teenage sons, my parents, and later Bob's son, and Bob. It was an ongoing effort using my time and energies.

There was also the personal search for identity and eventually an overwhelming yearning to spend my working days in a place other than the sheltered work setting for retarded adults, my penultimate employment. Despite having grown to love the clients individually, I had burnt out working with this population. There was no future for me. As things were, there was no fulfillment of my need to feel challenged, or for that matter appreciated in any way. The monotony of setting up and supervising an assembly line and lack of opportunity for advancement made me feel futile and took a toll on my psyche. After many years, I no longer felt that I was making a difference and found it most difficult to drive the ten miles to work without falling asleep at the wheel. Clearly, it was urgent that I get out.

Memories surfaced about discussions with friends regarding my options that came to naught, useless interviews with business people, and the feelings of inadequacy that were always my shadows. I had no hidden or visible talent for sales; whatever field I turned to, I had no experience to offer. In short, they were not looking for me. I felt trapped in my employment situation and saw no way to disentangle and move on.

The "filmstrip" of memories continues to the evening when I reluctantly accepted an invitation to join an acquaintance at a local meeting of "new singles."

I was particularly downhearted that day: fed up with a faltering relationship with a man who was leaving on weekends to be with another woman and not making any effort to continue our relationship, a difficult teen-aged son, and demanding, although loving and caring, parents. From the start, the evening didn't go well. I couldn't bring myself to join in or begin a conversation with anyone I greeted around the refreshment table. Everyone seemed to be heading in a direction away from me. I announced to my acquaintance my intention to leave. She persuaded me to stay a little longer.

"Have you said hello to Hohberg?" she asked, pointing to a ridiculously mustachioed (handlebar-style) skinny man in tight jeans, leather vest, a bolo tie, and cowboy boots, flitting about the room "mingling," being charming to everyone – the emcee this evening. I had not. I knew his name from ten years before when I had met Robert H at a party. I had noticed a middle-aged man who looked quite silly in a bizarre get-up; I had failed to recognize him. He had changed drastically from the last time I saw him.

Later in the evening, I caught his attention.

"Good evening Mr. H," I said. "Do you remember me? I was Gerry's wife."

He brightened. "Do I remember you? Are you kidding? You were the most elegant woman at Gerry's memorial service." He took me by the elbow and steered across the room to a row of empty chairs.

"Please, have a seat and don't move. I'll be right back." He disappeared into the crowd and I watched him flit around the room some more, smiling and bowing, making sure everyone was having a good time. I was thinking about his ridiculous get-up and wondered what motivated such excess. When he came back, we talked for three hours, catching up on what life had brought.

I finished brushing my teeth, turned off the bathroom light, and headed for bed.

"So, what happened next?" one might ask.

As unlikely as it may seem, that evening was the beginning of a mutually nurturing lifelong friendship, and years later a married partnership.

THE HATCHLINGS on the balcony

Something dark, strong, and fast came at me when I leaned the spout of the watering can over the pot of epiphyllum on the balcony. It hit me in the chest and flew away. I let out a startled yell and realized that a bird had taken up residence in the flowerpot and I had just frightened it as much as it frightened me. Two white, smooth, golf ball sized oval eggs were left where she had been. I regretted having disrupted the development of the potential family, but it happened; there was nothing I could do.

Later, I went to check, and sure enough the mourning dove had returned and resumed her job of sitting on her brood. All was well again, in her world and mine. From then on, I checked on her every day and spoke to her soothingly, asking how she was feeling, and commenting on the weather. It was the first time I ever spoke to an animal, feeling related, despite knowing that it was a one-way alliance. She let me get quite close and seemed at ease. The only change I noticed over the days was her position; she faced in different directions on different days and seemed to grow heftier. Then one day she was not there; two roundish grey feathery little beings were in her place. They lay cuddled together side by side. She came back and the following days they were still under her, but their heads were out, and their shiny, beady little eyes looking around the wall of the pot.

A few more days and their heads and the upper part of their bodies became visible. They were chubby and didn't have open beaks; nor was the mother actively coming and going to bring food. She was either gone or sat keeping them warm as they grew. There were no sounds coming from the pot. Everybody seemed content. I spoke to them daily as they grew, and their little heads were moving more to take in the scenery in the flower pot. Their mother seemed to sit higher as they got bigger. I never saw her fly away nor return, but in the evening, she was always there. I began to wonder how long they would be my guests and be content with the narrow world of the brown side of the flower pot.

One sunny morning, I found one of the birds in the same place it had been since it hatched, but the other was on the other side of the pot, evidently trying its legs and looking around. It walked around investigating the neighborhood looking over the rim of the pot, and suddenly hopped onto the lip of the vessel. It surveyed the world from this new vantage point walking about bobbing its head this way and that. I had a feeling that this was the day when it would try something new and life-changing. Action was in its demeanor. Flapping its wings twice, it walked some more, then flew the length of a doorway to a table at the edge of the balcony for more exploration.

I was watching all this time, fascinated by how this bird was self-guiding in preparation for life. It was taking one step at a time, ever closer to the goal of independence. When it felt secure, it flew another two feet and alit on the railing of the balcony, this time facing in the direction of the world, looking at trees, the road, a parking lot, and the freeway. It stayed for a few minutes checking out the next and final step to emancipation, opened its wings as wide as they would go and flew away.

The fellow hatchling lay quietly all this time. A moment later, it stood up in the flowerpot, spread its wings and flew purposefully out into the world. These two birds seemed to take on the world in individual ways. I wonder if that suggests that birds too have inherited individual personalities that manifest themselves from the moment they hatch?

THE INTERVIEW

My assignment from the editor of the local newspaper was to interview an elderly author about her methods of research, how she puts her works together, and what motivates her. It seemed like a routine assignment; I went to the retirement community where the lady lived. It had not occurred to me that I would emerge from our tete a tete changed and inspired.

The lady is of certain vintage, yet her attitude and enthusiasms are youthful. Her short, wavy silver-grey hair is "wash and wear," she says in response to my comment that it's pretty. She wears no make-up, the sparkle in her dark eyes makes up for it, and her classically-styled casual, outfit tells of a woman who liked clothes.

The walls of her sunny apartment are filled with paintings of landscapes, flowers, and still-lives. It's cheery and the view of sky and surrounding mountains is magnificent.

"Come in, come in," she beckons. "I have a story to tell you even before you ask any questions." She is obviously excited about something she wants to share and indicates a couch for me to sit on, so she can begin.

"One evening in late October, when it's dark by five o'clock, I'm on my way to dinner. An old man is walking ahead of me in the long corridor. His dejection shows in the stoop of his shoulders, the way his eyes seem to be burrowing into the floor in front of him, and the tight, down-turned curve of his mouth.

"'Hello, going to dinner?' I ask in passing, just to let him know that I'm there, so he won't get startled as I go by on the soft carpeting that makes us all walk silently.

"'Yes, I guess so,' he grumbles in a hoarse, aged voice as dispirited as his appearance. His head is imposing: thick white hair surrounds his weatherworn, large-featured face in which his nose and ears are most prominent; he might be a former statesman or politician. Judging from his physique, he was once tall, broad shouldered, and athletic. Now, somewhat shrunken physically by age and disuse of muscles, and emotionally by the recent loss of his wife he is but a shell of his former self. The sadness in his voice makes me feel compassionate and want to be of help. I stop momentarily and turn back to look at him; he oozes despondency.

"The empty place left by the loss of my own *other half* is still fresh, and I want to offer consolation to a fellow griever. I search my mind for something kind to say, anything, but what? To my astonishment, I hear myself say,

"'Are you meeting someone, or would you like to join me for dinner?'

"'Yes, I would like that,' he answers slowly, lifting his gaze from where it was focused near the floor. His voice is flat, tired. We walk the rest of the length of the corridor to the dining room together and check in at the host desk.

"He seems to be waiting for me to lead. My eyes roam around the room for a partially occupied table to join other residents, but there is none. I find an available table for four, allowing for space for anyone else that might be looking for company to join us. *I don't want to dine solo with this very cheerless man.*

"At the moment, we're alone together. He makes no effort at conversation and it appears that it might be a silent meal. I'm sociable and talkative by nature so I start introducing myself.

"'I know who you are,' he interrupts. "My wife and I had dinner with you when we first moved in." Then silence.

"To attempt conversation, I ask, 'Did you know many people here before you came?"

"'No, not anyone, really.'

"'Where did you live before? Are you from far away?' I ask to encourage him to speak some more.

"'Well, not really very far, just about fifteen miles north of here.'

"'Is that where you spent your life?'

"'Not all of it. Before that, we lived in the San Fernando Valley." His need or desire for conversational interaction is clearly low to non-existent. I try again.

"'How long have you been living here?'

"'Oh, since January.'

"I calculate that means about ten months. To fill the silence that follows, I thought I'd give him the benefit of my experience with the facility and its customs.

"'Maybe I should tell you, now that you're on your own, that you need to make sure you mingle with people daily for your mental and physical health. Come out to the dining room for at least one meal a day and join a table where one or two residents are seated, and empty places are available.'

"He seems to be listening, but there is no verbal reaction, nor change in affect. I continue.

"'It's also important that you join in activities to interact with people. It gives you a chance to be part of the community. As a male in a predominantly female world, you'll be quite welcome and in demand as a dinner companion.'

"His gaze is fixed on my face while I hold forth, but he doesn't say anything; and a little ill at ease, I keep talking.

"'Another important thing is that you take your meals with different people each day. That'll keep you from being fodder for the very active gossip mill. You don't want to be paired in peoples' minds, and it happens very quickly in a place like this."

"His heavy-lidded, luminous grey eyes are totally focused on me, but he doesn't respond; he seems to be listening, but his expression doesn't betray any hint of what he thinks of my well-intentioned words of good advice. By the end of the meal, his demeanor is more cheerful, and I know he is pleased.

"He has told me a little about his life; that he was born in a tiny town in Nebraska. The family relocated to California in 1937, after a tornado wiped out much of their town. His wartime service was in the Philippines, followed by a solid marriage of 61 years to the girl from the next farm. The social life of the family was deeply involved with the church and its communal activities. They traveled in groups by camper in the United States and he made European forays to visit his son in the armed forces. By this time, I feel tired, as if I had to pry these nuggets from a vein in a rock.

"After dinner, I wish him a pleasant rest of the evening, say good night, and leave, feeling good about having reached out to someone so obviously down in the dumps. I had shared some of the things I've learned in the process of facing life as a widow and think it may help him pick up the pieces faster.

"Well, the following evening, on the way to dinner, he's waiting for me in the hallway! This is not what I meant when I advised him to mingle with the residents. I wondered if he had been listening the previous evening. Did I fail to explain the realities of a place like this clearly? He's determined to join me for dinner. With some polite words of mild rebuke, I agree to dine together a second time and select a table, making sure extra places are available. No one joins us.

"In an effort to draw him out of his silence, I ask questions about his life and times and regale him with stories about mine. He responds with minimal facts in short sentences; one would characterize him as a typical, monosyllabic Yankee. In answer to any question that may involve an opinion, his phrases usually begin with 'that depends on…' and end without having divulged anything but facts, betraying nothing that might remotely verge on a feeling or opinion about any issue.

"On my arrival on the third evening, the host at the dining room tells me, 'Mr. X isn't here yet…. Uh oh! I've already been paired, even by the staff. That is not what I wanted, although it's interesting that two dinners are all it takes for the young servers to consider us as an *item*.

"During the next two months, he always appears in the hallway to intercept me on the way to dinner. One evening, I mention the Christmas lights display at the Wild Animal Park, and how much I enjoy seeing such things. He suggests we go and I agree.

"We visit the Wild Animal Park together after dark in early January. He is having a difficult evening; frequent visits to the toilet facilities. It's chilly and damp. The dark-clad forms in the dimly lit area are difficult to distinguish. My anxiety increases every time he goes to the men's room. I think, what if he's ill? How will we get home if he can't drive?

"He says, 'I feel so embarrassed… so sorry…our first date and all…"

"'Oh, no, no… don't worry about any of that. This is *not* a date.

We're *neighbors*,' I say, hoping to dispel his discomfort. Dating is not part of my thinking now. My immediate concern is with feeling helpless if something serious were the matter with him and getting us both home safely.

"Trying to see through the murkiness of the dim lighting is difficult, except right under the street lamps where it's bright, and I feel insecure walking on the bumpy terrain. I take a chance and say, 'Do you mind if I hold on to your hand, so we don't get separated in this darkness? I don't have a good sense of direction and have no desire to get lost here.'

"I reach for him. His hand is warm, and his grasp is firm. It feels surprisingly good. It's a risky moment. I wonder if he thinks I'm being too forward and am asking myself if it was a mistake to mention the lights in the first place. To my relief, we got home safely."

*****

By this time, I was so interested in the old lady's personal story that I'd forgotten why I had come. Oh, yes! It was to do a brief profile about her. She must have noticed me shift my position because she quickly said, "Wait, I'm almost finished."

"Okay, so then what happened?" I'm intrigued and want to hear more.

"Well, there are times when we're together, I feel as if I am young in my head, but old in my body. You'd be surprised, my dear, how a little romance can distract from one's aches and pains. It's the most wonderful antidote for pain and worry."

"Sounds like an elixir. Where can I buy a bottle?" I ask.

"The body calls me a liar by zinging me with arthritic pain. No matter, I still feel 30 years younger. There's nothing one can drink to stave off aging, but these new sensations reduce the feelings of being old. Since that first dinner and the evening outing to see the lights at the Wild Animal Park, there have been shared days, romantic nights, and trips around the country. We've developed trust, intimacy, and deep caring for one another. It's a new adventure that adds meaning to each day. We accept losses, pain, and accommodate with a new equanimity schedules at doctors' offices that the aging process requires. A smile of appreciation, a chuckle, or a heartfelt laugh at a joke makes it all worthwhile.

"It must be getting late, and I don't want to keep you here overtime. I've so enjoyed sharing this little story. It's a joy to make a bereaved person smile and to be appreciated and loved in return. Starting that evening in November, there is new excitement and a sense of mission in my life. Incongruously, the feelings are those of *a young lover*, but without the uncertainties. To quote a very old song, 'What a difference a day makes.'

"So, there's a story for you. Hope you can use it."

THOUGHTS IN A WAITING ROOM

I interviewed a lady who was born in 1902. That made her 102 years old. In my mind, it triggered visions of bustles, hoop skirts, corsets, high button shoes, large over-decorated hats, and sun bonnets, as well as streets filled with horses and wagons and then trolley tracks. She was born before my father.

That set me to thinking about members of my family's birthdates; to compare the world of my grandparents and my parents with my own time from the standpoint of technology, fashion, and attitudes.

Focusing on the math proved to be a boon in the waiting room of a dental surgeon's office, where my husband was undergoing a major oral operation. I was trying to calm myself from the worry and anxiety I was experiencing. My restless mind alit on the subject that the interview had stirred, and I started doing the math regarding the possible birth dates of my grandparents and their siblings. It was a good way to fill my mind with structure to help me through the fretting concerns of the moment.

I began with my paternal grandmother, who died when I was just a year old. I recall that my father said she was only 54. She would have been born in approximately 1885; she would have been part of the change-over of technology to the common use of the telephone, telegraph, and automobile. In fashion, my grandma went from a bustle and corset complemented by a large-brimmed hat adorned with peacock or ostrich feathers, and high button shoes, to a more unencumbered style, and may even have tried on a short, narrow, flapper dress, transparent silk stockings, and pumps. She also lived into the beginning of the age of commercial flight.

My paternal grandfather had come to the United States as a teenager in the late 1890s. He returned to Austria, married, established a beer import and distribution business, and had three children. He built a four-story building with a cobble stone courtyard that accommodated a barn for the horses and wagon for making deliveries as well as a garage for the Buick. Along with his daughter and grandchildren, he was exterminated in 1942, in the ovens at Belzec, one of the most notorious, but rarely mentioned, death camps in Poland. By my count, my grandparents were born about 120 years ago.

My other grandparents have different parentheses around their lives. If Grandpa was in his 50s in 1939, he would have been born in early 1880s and a young man in World War I. He was deported to Siberia when the Russo-German Pact was broken in WWII, jailed there briefly without charges in 1942, and released. Later, the reason for the incarceration was said to have been his hiring the help of two young men to chop wood to store for the winter. Evidently, paying for a service was considered an act of punishable bourgeois exploitation in the "Communist" perception of the time.

Of pensioner age, he and my grandmother were later taken to a retirement home in Saratov by the Soviets, as an entitlement for older people. They both survived and returned to Poland after the end of WWII. They witnessed the creation of the State of Israel in 1948, and in the early 1950s managed to fulfill their wish to go there. They lived in a room in a pension in Haifa on Mt. Carmel. I don't know when Grandpa Moses died, how old he was, or the cause of death. Grandma was living at the pension when my mother and I made our pilgrimage to see her in 1954. She died the following year. I remember hearing 77 as her age at death. That means that she may have been born in 1877.

Not only did she experience the bustle, the corset, and the large hat, but she lived through the cruelest persecution of her people, the numbing cold of Siberia, and the dawn of the atomic age. She saw the advent of routine international commercial flight by an official Israeli Airline that must have been a great source of pride.

These ruminations helped me focus my attention on something less worrisome than what my husband was going through, and I gained a deeper understanding of the world in which my immediate forebears lived and thought.

TIME ... some thoughts

Time... Time is an important element in all the areas of the globe inhabited by humans. Centuries ago a standard we call hours that are subdivided into smaller units was created and is followed universally.

Time isn't tangible or real in a concrete sense – it can't be touched or felt. Yet it's measured and valued. In the professions, its units often carry a higher value than in manual labor industries. We can't see it or touch it, yet we live by it; much of our orientation depends on it. Our sense of worth is often tied to how much of something we can accomplish in how little time. We arrange to meet, to catch trains and planes and boats by it. Goods and services are delivered with time as a reference point.

Calendars divide time into segments significant to specific communities and to the world at large. In many third world countries, and even within industrialized ones, sub-groups exist that function on their own time with respect to religious observance, or political anniversaries. People within families or communities sometimes have ritual times all their own. Historically, dictatorial types sometimes try to institute a new order by reckoning time from the beginning of their reign.

Expression of the passage of time isn't always reckoned in hours, or even days; in unindustrialized countries, it's often defined by the temperature characteristic of a season as, for instance, "when it's colder," or the birth or death of an important person, "when grandpa was born," or a major event, such as "when the sun became dark at mid-day" that affected the community at large.

On the international level, it was agreed to divide the globe into longitudinal time zones from Greenwich, England going east and West. The agreement has been holding for hundreds of years and has been of incalculable help to commerce and general communication of time-related issues.

For me time is the reference system by which I manage to do things important and otherwise. It sustains me in times of stress to know that it will pass, or elation to anticipate that an event will occur at a predetermined time. Despite time being an abstract concept, it governs, if not enslaves us. Its structure is accepted by the entire "civilized" world.

There are several phrases often used to indicate some aspect in which time might play a role: "I didn't have enough time…" as if it were yard goods. "I can't find the time…" as if it were hiding. "If time permits" …suggesting that it has the power to give such permission. There are many idioms that allude to time as a noun with concrete properties, such as "time on my hands," "the river of time" and others. "We may have enough time…" Is there a standard measure of "enough?" The common: "Let's get together sometime" generally meaning "probably or preferably never" is an oft -heard phrase.

Just about everything we partake of and communicate has a dependency on an element of time.

Isn't it amazing, that in a world torn by continuous and ever more vicious strife because we humans are too greedy and don't communicate well enough to get along, we have universally agreed to accept that an hour is sixty minutes long?

TIMES OF DAY

Morning.
It is dark.
The sound of traffic intensifies as
the light behind the mountain
grows larger and brighter with every wondrous moment,
spreading its brilliance and warmth over the world.
Thousands of crows flit across my field of vision
on their way to their day jobs.
Sunrise, the beginning of another day.
Midday.
The sun is high,
the shadows short,
Hunger stirs inside me,
It must be noontime.
Night.
The reflected glow of sun disappears behind the mountain,
its brilliant light suffusing the sky;
Hosts of crows,
black cut-outs in the turquoise-and-orange-streaked sunset
fly to their roosting branches in trees.
Darkness falls quickly.

TO TRUST OR NOT?

On a recent visit to Urgent Care facility with a painful left hip and knee, the doctor sent an orderly to the room to take me to x-ray. I was placed in a wheel chair for the trundle a few doors down the hall. There, I told the tech emphatically that my left hip needs looking at. She agreed and prepared me on the table making sure my right side was properly aligned and put some sort of a sticker on it. I repeated that it was my left that was today's main concern.

"Yes, I know," she said. While she was making sure that all was in order, I explained that I'm deliberate in mentioning my left side because I often hear of mistakes. She agreed that many are made. She assured me that there was room for both hips to show on the x-ray. When ready, she told me to hold my breath, went to her machine, and activated it to take the picture.

"Okay, now you can breathe normally," she announced. "I'll be right back."

She left the room. When she came back, she told me that the picture was of the right hip, and that she would have to re-take it because the doctor made a mistake. She did the procedure over.

Back in the doctor's exam room, I asked what's going on. He said she made a mistake. In fact, she had the wrong patient.

How is one to trust?

UNUSUAL ENCOUNTER

I am waiting for the elevator in my building. An elderly woman with a wrinkled face, heavily made-up smiling eyes, and intensely light blonde hair is standing next to me. I have never seen her before and we're both obviously waiting to go up. I wonder if she's a visitor or perhaps a new resident, and venture to ask.

"Hello. Are you visiting or a new resident?"

"Yes, I live here. And you?" she answered in heavily accented English.

"Welcome, my name is Ruth, and you are…?"

"Wiltrud. They call me Willie."

"Ah…! Welcome to Casa. Are you Danish, Dutch, or German?" I left the German option for last, sensing that was the right one.

"German."

"Ah, so, do you still speak it?"

"Yes, but right now, I'm reading a most wonderful book in English. It's by a Jewish lady who writes about her experiences in WWII. You know, getting out of Europe, and things. Awful thing but a wonderful book."

"Do you know her name or the name of the book?" I ask ready to try to make a note to look it up.

"Her name is Ruth… I can't remember the last name."

"Is it Ruth Gruber? She has written a number of interesting books about that time."

"No, it's something with an H… Hober, or maybe something like that. It's a great book, you should try it."

I'm beginning to feel that this conversation isn't real. Can this be happening to me? I'm not sure what to say but am thrilled to pieces if she really means it.

"Is it Ruth Hohberg?" I ask tentatively.

"Yes! That's it! That's her name!!!"

"You're looking at her. That's me!"

She opens her arms and hugs me tightly. "I'm so delighted to have met you!"

We're on the fourth floor and go our separate ways. I feel much taller than I was on the first floor.

WEDDING IN WARTIME

I must have been nine-years-old that summer when I saw a wedding in wartime Uzbekistan. The marriage united a Russian man with the buxom young blonde who lived with her mother across the stream.

The stream that separated our homes carried the waste products of man and beast, and was the same one in which we bathed, washed our dishes and our clothes, and was the source of our water for drinking and cooking. It flowed by the side of the dried clay brick structure in which we lived.

On this special day, I had a good vantage point to observe some of the proceedings from the far side of the creek, and to hear the goings-on.

As seems to be tradition worldwide, the bride wearing something white and the groom in his best outfit posed for a picture outdoors with trees as a backdrop. The photographer, a European, who always wore a pre-war fedora lived next door to the bride and was the only person in the village of one thousand who had a camera. The camera was a box-like affair mounted on a large wooden tripod covered with a black cloth. It looked mysterious and magical. He slid what looked like a metal plate into the side of it, instructed the young couple where to stand, smile, and stay very still. Then he ducked his head under the cloth, held up one hand, and pouf! A light flashed. He reappeared from under the cloth, pulled the plate out, put it in a bag, folded his tripod, replaced the hat on his head, and left.

Tables and chairs were set out on the flat space on the bank of the creek. As the food and drink prepared by the women were being enjoyed by the guests, the noise level of their singing became louder, more strident, ever more slurred, and eventually a fight broke out between two men, then another joined the fray. I watched from across the creek spellbound and frightened of what the fight might lead to. I was hoping nobody would be thrown into the water or seriously hurt. The drunken voices became more menacing and the sound of the impact when the men slugged each other was awful. The women seemed to be taking this behavior in stride, bringing more food to the tables, and cleaning up the mess left by the men as they became more inebriated and raucous.

After a while I ran inside, not wanting to be witness to any more. This was too scary.

The festivities lasted for several days, although the number of carousers diminished in energy as time passed. The big day was over, and married life for the couple began. They moved away soon after. Sometimes I wonder how their lives played out, and what they told their children about that day when they showed them the old picture.

WHEN IT'S OVER

School was out for the summer. Rebecca and Zach's two sons, Ronnie, 16, and Donnie, 10, their belongings packed, were ready to leave for camp. Ronnie would be away for two weeks in Massachusetts at lacrosse, while Don and his trumpet were to spend 4 weeks at the New England Music Camp in Maine. On this morning, the boys were to meet their respective buses and be given over to the temporary custody of camp counselors.

Rebecca was looking forward to the hiatus from managing the sibling rivalry that had a way of always leading to disagreement between Zach and her. Zachary was in the habit of taking an opposite position regardless of what Rebecca said, making life a verbally contentious, emotionally stressful battlefield. She expected to have some quiet time alone with Zach while the boys were at camp, hoping they would make this time an opportunity to talk things out and set a course for their family's future well-being by being more communicative with each other. She had envisioned open and honest conversations or discussions to lessen the emotional distance between them without Zach feeling he had to use clever techniques of making her feel in the wrong, and "proving" her ineptitude at every turn. She hoped to bring back to their consciousness why they had married in the first place, and to restore a long-abandoned goal of togetherness. In recent years, they had not spoken to one another except about the basic utilitarian needs of a household; was dinner ready, had the trash been taken out, had the dog been walked and fed, and the occasional comment about the weather. There were no personal exchanges that might have resembled conversations between married people or even better, good friends.

They didn't speak on the drive home. Rebecca harbored the fantasy of a relaxed breakfast a deux and maybe a chat that would not end in recriminations. She was aching to use this break in routine to help bring them closer. She desperately wanted to be able to take this time to articulate the issues that had arisen to separate them, and that they would find their way back to the hopes they had for their married life.

Now, after 17 years, they were much further apart than she could ever have imagined.

Back home in the kitchen, she put breakfast on the table.

"Hurry up with those eggs, and make sure they're the way I want them. You never make them right," Zach said as he sat down. His facial expression told her there would most likely be no conversation, and certainly no rapprochement. When she sat down at the opposite end of the table she took a long look at him. He was looking at his plate.

Zach wasn't a talkative person, but when he said something to hurt, it packed a punch one didn't forget.

"Are you trying to poison me adding salt to these eggs? The toast is too dark too, I'm not eating it, throw it away." After a little while of silence, he said, "And by the way, everyone in this town has a decent wife, only I don't. Why do you think that is?"

She felt as if struck with a cudgel. That was the coup de grace, the last straw. The image of the Rock of Gibraltar, Rebecca's metaphor for a good marriage had been chipped away piece by piece by Zach over the years. Now, the last piece had fallen into the sea and was gone. She had taken enough. It was over. The fantasy of building relationship was not to happen regardless of the constructive conversations in her head. The marriage was over, except in name.

PART II

MEMORIES THAT
STAND OUT

MEMORIES THAT STAND OUT

TABLE OF CONTENTS

FOREWORD

I was awake but not ready to start the day. It was still too dark, too early. I settled back into my bed for a while longer nuzzled into the pillow to enjoy its comfort while getting my thoughts together. Bits of memories began to float through my mind, without any chronology or theme. They just kept coming… I let them flow.

This is a collection of memory fragments of events decades ago, and of recent vintage, in no particular order. The trigger for a memory that pops up can be visual, auditory, or olfactory. I may notice something in passing or hear someone say something, and there it is full-blown. Other memories seem to appear "out of the blue" without my being consciously aware of the stimulus. Reading something often has the same effect, and I wonder what factor in our makeup it is that reaches back in time so instantly to bring these recollections back with such vivid force and such speed.

THE BARN

I recalled a day in 1942 when I was seven. After spending the winter as political prisoners in a Siberian labor camp, my family was traveling in a cattle car on the way south to what we hoped was a warmer climate. Soldiers boarded the train in the middle of nowhere and we were unceremoniously ejected into the chilly, rainy day.

We found ourselves in a village in Uzbekistan as part of forcible resettlement of populations. It was a primitive pastoral setting, at least looking back in time seventy plus years later, after having lived in cities and experienced the high decibel levels of sound and the pace of advanced technologies, dense population, and modern architecture.

It was a clear, sunny day when we moved into our new home, a barn that we were to have for that summer while the owner's cow was out to pasture. We had just arranged our one suitcase and our bundles as furniture, and had carefully placed the cot, our one piece of almost-real furniture where we thought it would fit best. I was outdoors exploring the new environment around the little clay brick structure when I heard a terrible noise above me quickly getting louder and more frightening. I looked up and saw an object; the huge wing of a low-flying plane obscured the sun for a moment. I ran screaming into the barn and crouched behind the suitcase in terror. My mother had a hard time convincing me that we would not be bombed here and that I shouldn't worry.

The shadow passed swiftly, the noise dissipating in the distance. All was peaceful again. It took much longer for me to recover from the fright.

Another day that same summer, my father came outside holding a small flat round glass with a handle that we had brought from Europe in one hand and a piece of old newspaper in the other. It was a magnifying glass and I asked what he was doing. He said he was going to make a fire to light his cigarette that was made from dried broken up leaves and rolled into a little square of newspaper.

He held the glass close to the paper at a certain angle to concentrate the heat from the sun on it, until the heat ignited the paper; intriguing.

He gave me a talk on how dangerous it is to smoke and said I mustn't ever get the habit because it makes people sick and they die. I pleaded for a taste of the cigarette until he relented; I liked the taste. He warned me again.

Many years later, in my teens, I smoked a cigarette on the way to the subway station in the mornings, to impress myself and, hopefully, passersby by my pretense of sophistication. Did anyone notice? Probably not.

PLAYING WITH FIRE

Another flame and heat-related memory is of an event that took place when I was ten. The origin of the idea is lost in the mists of time, but the results are clear. Someone had told me about Polish scientist Mme. Curie, and somewhere I heard that sand and high heat are needed to make glass. My curiosity was aroused. I had hidden two sleek glass ampoules filled with ether in my jacket pocket some months before, when we emptied a little steel box first-aid kit acquired at the start of the war. Now the box was needed for anti-malaria pills my mother had to distribute to the natives as part of her job. She had instructed me emphatically to throw them away, but I thought them too pretty.

Those bits of unconnected information gave me an idea. Late on the evening of January 10, 1945, I noticed a loose button on my jacket. I gave the jacket to my mother to sew it back on. Fearful of being scolded for having kept the ampoules, I took them from the pocket. I held their smooth shapes lovingly in my hand; the fire was bright in the little iron open stove stoked with "mazut," the shiny, black, gooey substance, a by-product of petroleum that we used to warm our tiny closet of a room.

It seemed the perfect opportunity to see the melting process, but parting from the precious little shapes forever was hard. I stared at the brilliant yellows and blues as they curled and wound and subsided as others formed; making my decision, I tossed the ampoules in. My attention and anticipation were concentrated on the dancing bright yellow flames, as I watched, expecting to see my little treasures melt. Instead, the ether in the ampoules exploded and hot black mazut splashed all over, covering my face causing a severe burn. I assume the glass was so thin that we never found bits of it.

I won't go into the story of the immediate aftermath. The real nightmare came during the following week when, swathed in a mask of sheep's fat mixed with sulfur, courtesy of Ida Salomonovna, my personal healing angel from Odessa to heal my burn, I came down with a case of chicken pox. The itch was unbelievable. Despite the curative salve and my mother's best efforts, I scratched a spot over my lip and bear the scar for life.

THE SHORTENED SALAMI

Several weeks after our group of deportees had been deposited in the remote part of Siberia, the year's High Holidays came.

I can see my five-year-old self, looking at the table where we were all having supper a few minutes before. My intense focus was on the length of salami and the knife left on the table when the grownups went out for a clandestine, illegal prayer service. I was left in the cabin by myself and, of course, told to behave - whatever that meant.

I was not sated, and the tempting smell of the sausage lying there, just asking to be eaten, was too much to resist. I looked at it for a while, plotting how to have some without it being noticed when the family returned, and decided to cut a very thin slice. That worked. I cut another, and another, and the salami still looked the same size as before. I was pleased with my skill; my taste buds and my stomach were very happy.

When the family returned, Grandma asked, "What happened to the salami? It was much longer when we left."

Her gaze and her words were directed at me. I said nothing. I didn't have to say anything. She knew, and she let me know that she knew by telling me about the all- knowing God who sees everything and knows everything that goes on in your mind.

That may have been the first lesson regarding even thinking about lying. I wasn't sure whether this God really knew and saw everything, but why take chances?

I grew up telling the truth.

A MITTEN

When I was four-and-a-half years old, my family and I were caught up in the insanity that reigned in Europe at the beginning of and during WWII. We were part of the populations living near the German border that Stalin, the dictator of the Soviet Union, thought might threaten his armies by embracing the Nazi ideology. Because of his paranoia, he ordered large segments of the population to be rounded up without warning, arrested, declared Enemies of the People, and deported to far-flung and desolate places in his empire.

After traveling north in a cattle car for four weeks, we arrived somewhere away from everything, in the middle of nothing. It must have been October or later; it was much colder than where we had left. Winter was setting in. We were herded out of the train into waiting trucks.

It was a long, bumpy ride through the forest before the truck stopped and we were ordered out into a very empty landscape. I remember seeing only a log cabin on a slight rise and the exhausted, hungry, and chilled group of deportees in summer clothes being directed with hand signals by the Russian-speaking soldiers already wearing their winter uniforms. When the snow came, we were marooned in whiteness, 150-miles from the nearest railroad station, for the duration of a famous Siberian winter.

One of the most damaging things that can happen in such intense cold is to have an uncovered body part exposed for any length of time. At worst, it can result in the loss of digits or limbs, or… don't even want to think about it.

I was playing in the snow on a flat part at the top of a small hill near our cabin, from where a path led down to the river, frozen solid now. I realized that one hand felt colder than the other; my mitten was gone! This was a major calamity, as we had no materials to replace such an important piece of protection. I searched as long as the short daylight allowed; I hoped that, if I could just tell my father he would come to help me look, and we would certainly find it; then all would be well. I didn't want my mother to know. I already knew that she was excitable and would scold ferociously. I didn't like to be yelled at. It didn't help. I could rely on my father to stay calm and not spend time with remonstrations.

We combed the snowy area while more snow was falling and went back empty-handed to face my mother, who pointed out, in her despair, that this was only the beginning of a winter that would probably not be over until May. It was a sad end to what was to be a nice day with the kids. I don't recall how my hand was saved with only frostbite on my fingers, but no loss of digits.

THINKING GROWNUP

I see myself at 7 years of age in Uzbekistan, at the door of our room in the one-level building where rooms lined both sides of the corridor. My father was at work.

My mother had a very high fever and men with a stretcher came to take her to the hospital. They carried her out to a waiting cart that had two very tall wheels powered by a donkey, then departed down the unpaved road to the health facility. The cart moved away, becoming quite small in the distance as I watched it go.

Suddenly, I was on my own, unprepared to be so. What to do?

I made the decision to take matters in my own hands, went back to the room, and began being my own "boss." No one to allow or forbid anything. I took my only dress, one that came from America in a distribution program, and put it on. It was red, green, blue, and white, in a lively paisley design, had short puff sleeves, and buttons down the front; very pretty and I felt quite "in charge."

I picked up the large ball of yarn my mother and I had made by unraveling long, American army-issue underwear for the wool. It was so Mother would knit a sweater that would hopefully be sold to help our economic situation. I dropped it on the floor, it bounced beautifully. Not having a ball to play with, this would temporarily make up for it. I blissfully sauntered down the corridor, feeling authoritative and pretty, wearing my finery and bouncing my new toy. A Russian neighbor spotted me and administered a thorough upbraiding, questioning my sense of consideration and responsibility, making me feel quite guilty.

In the evening, I prepared supper for my father and he knew nothing of my escapade. Added to my mother's mantra, "duty before pleasure," and now her illness, the day made a powerful impact. I conducted myself with more dignity and decorum ever after.

Much weakened, my mother returned home several days later. She regained her strength slowly and we resumed our lives as best we could.

BREAD RATION CARDS

Remembering that early display of "carelessness" in losing a mitten in the snow reminded me of an event later, when I was 7, an age that is generally thought of in America as carefree childhood. At the time, we were in a different part of the world, in Central Asia, in Uzbekistan. Over a period of 4 years, while I was growing older, the powers that had us under their control transported us to several living arrangements.

Altaryk, a village in the Fergana valley is similar in climate to parts of California. It winter, it gets rainy and raw - a chill goes through the bones. We were settled into a room in a dormitory-style building where families lived in cubicles, with a window and a door, that lined both sides of a long corridor. Plumbing, heating, and electricity were the stuff of fantasy. To light the twigs we collected for cooking, a family member, usually a child, had to go around the village to see if there was smoke, if anyone had a flame, and then bring it home on a twig to light the fire. Life had to be managed as best one could. Bread ration cards were distributed at the beginning of each month. I was put in charge of ours and responsible for picking up our daily portion.

Toward the end of the sugar cane harvest season, a few of us children were in the field, picking what was left of the succulent canes, breaking them, and twisting the juice out into our mouths. Perhaps they were left to obey the exhortation in the Bible to always leave some of the harvest behind for those in need.

The weather was wintry, the air had a bite to it, and the field looked desolate, bare except for a few canes sticking up here and there. We were dragging some canes along as we walked and talked, and I remembered that I was to do the bread errand. Reaching for the ration card I found the pocket empty.

At age seven, I was old enough to know that this was a catastrophe. It was the first week of the month and the card was essential to provide my family with bread. I retraced my steps in the field looking carefully all around the ground. Nothing. I was in a panic and didn't know what to do. I waited to tell my father what had happened, and he and I walked the field again. We found nothing and went back to my mother with the bad news. True to form, she exhausted herself scolding me and then in her despair declared, "God will provide."

Somehow, we got through the extra hungry month. Maybe my mother was right.

NIGHT OF BROKEN DISHES

Feeling nauseated, tired, and having no sense of even wanting a future, I lay in the upper bunk of a Tourist Class cabin on the *SS Drottningholm*, bound from Goteborg, Sweden, to New York. It was mid-March of 1947. I was 12 years old and terribly seasick. My mother, excited by the prospect of the new, insisted I join her on deck.

"Come breathe some fresh sea air. You'll see. You'll feel much better."

An obedient child, I did as I was told. The steep and narrow metal stairs with high risers I had to climb to get there were difficult to negotiate in my misery.

I had never seen the sea before, nor had an inkling of how it might be. This was my first voyage and, parenthetically, 70 years later, I still would not wish the experience on anyone. We were traveling across the Atlantic on the first available berth to make our long-awaited home in America.

When we boarded our ship, it seemed quite large. I didn't imagine that when a storm arose it would be tossed around as if it were a toy, not the handsome vessel guided by what I thought of as a dignified captain and powered by great-big engines. The waves seemed to fling us high up, change direction abruptly like a yo-yo, rise again and drop. When I thought there would be a lull in the motion and I could collect my stomach, there wasn't. Before I could catch my breath, we were lifted, suspended for a split second, and dropped again. Endlessly, the ship heaved and swayed, and rolled, and pitched and yawed. The crashing of waves on the ship's sides made the structures creak so loudly that I expected the wall of my bunk to break through at any moment.

Standing on my wobbly legs on deck, clinging to an upright part of the ship, I watched the crew chase the chairs careening across the deck, so they could tie them down and save them from being blown overboard; I saw the horizon move from somewhere above, to somewhere below me. That really roiled my innards. The heavy pewter grey sky, rain, and high winds buffeting us were no help.

At night, when I lay in my bunk, holding onto the edge not to fall out, feeling ill and hopeless, the howling wind continued to blow and the waves to pound the sides. It felt as if the ship would be torn to bits of floating splinters by the constant and relentless rising and dropping into troughs between waves.

One night, the regular rhythmic sound from below the cabin, where the engines were, stopped suddenly; a lighter, slower beat replaced it. I awoke and heard the thwack of the waves and wondered what had happened, imagining the worst. I thought for sure we were done for.

Suddenly, the comparative stillness was broken by a loud, intense clatter outside the cabin, but nearby. After some minutes, it died down gradually, with a few more, wider-spaced sounds of breaking china before it stopped. I was too sick to care what it was and didn't get off my bunk to find out. I just lay there, holding on.

All the ship's dishes and cutlery that had been set in the dining room for breakfast slid off the tables and the dishes broke. In the morning, announcement was made that the captain had ordered the engines to be run at lowered power not to buck the winds but to let the ship ride it out. That accounted for the change in the rhythm. He felt it was the safest action he could take to preserve the integrity of the vessel at the time. I was happy to be alive and vowed never to go to sea again.

Note: During that storm that lasted several days, the *Queen Mary* the 1,132-foot British flagship, passed the 538-foot *Drottningholm*. Her size was almost eight times larger than ours and her speed proportionately faster. Later, it was announced that that she limped into port in New York Harbor with 23-injured passengers. We were very proud of our bark having brought all of us safely into harbor.

THE AUTOMAT

Among the first-week-in-New-York experiences was following Cousin Lola's suggestion that we take our lunch at the Horn and Hardart Automat, an eatery a longish-walk down 72nd Street near a very busy intersection of Broadway. She showed us the American coins and explained the value of each. One cent is the only copper coin, 5 cents called a nickel is larger, 10 cents is smallest of the coins, very shiny silver, and called a dime. The largest is 25 cents, called a quarter; it, too, is silver. When I looked at them more closely, I noticed their identifying images; they were quite interesting. One cent or a penny was the profile of Lincoln on one side. There were two versions of the nickel: one showing the profile of Jefferson on one side and a building on the other, and the other had the profile of an Indian in a feather headdress on one side and a buffalo on the obverse. The dime was smallest of all the coins. It was distinguished by its profile of Mercury with wings on his helmet.

Inside the restaurant, closest to the door, was a glass-enclosed booth where customers passed their dollar bills to the clerk on duty through a little opening, and received nickels, dimes, and quarters in return with what seemed to me like lightning speed.

One whole wall was covered with little framed windows; each had a handle. A sandwich or other item of food was displayed in each. There were many choices: sandwiches, casseroles, pasta dishes, and desserts; I think there were also fresh apples. The description and price of the item was printed clearly on a label on the outside. One made one's selection, put the requisite number of coins into a slot. It unlocked automatically, the door released, and one would remove the food. Cutlery and condiments were available on a separate table. This was very helpful to those of us not speaking English. There was no need to speak and one didn't have to go hungry. For me, not speaking any English and being very shy, it was a boon. Another advantage was that one could stay as long as one wished, meet friends, and relax. It was very exciting at first to have so many choices, and only turn the handle to get ready-to-eat wholesome food. We followed that regimen until my father arrived. Then it was time for us to move from the cousin's luxurious Central Park West setting to something of our own.

DRUGSTORE or drug store?

During our first week in New York, my mother and I took many walks down 72nd Street, along the stretch from Central Park West where the famous Dakota was across the street from 'our' building. Many celebrities were said to call it home. We looked at store windows, learned to figure out which way was up or downtown, and got a general sense of the city that "never sleeps."

I found out that, contrary to our thinking that a drug store sells only medications, the drugstores in America also sell postage stamps, maps, greeting cards, cosmetics, and hundreds of other items, including packaged foods, chocolates, candies, books, and magazines. They even have soda fountains where one can sit on a high stool and have a snack and a drink. Later, my father bought me a box camera at Whelan's Drugstore.

THE ROOM ON 68TH STREET

After my father arrived on April 7, 1947, it was time to move out of the luxurious accommodations at the cousin's and find our own. We had been told that housing was difficult to find because soldiers were returning, and immigrants displaced by the war were coming in great numbers. It was especially difficult to be accepted as a renter with a child.

My uncle recommended we go to the Whitehall Hotel at Broadway and 100th Street. He said it would be adequate for us while we looked around and figured things out. We rented a room furnished with the bare necessities: a sink, a dresser, and a rather tall bed I had to climb onto. The toilet was in the hallway.

During the first night, I got a rude awakening when I rolled off onto the floor. My parents saw this wasn't as adequate as my uncle thought and decided to look for something more suitable right away. A permanent address was a priority so that I could go to school.

Outside the hotel building, folks who were traumatized by what they had been through to survive the recently ended war, stood around at all hours; a ragged, sad-looking lot. My parents were looking for a healthier environment. We were advised to walk down the side streets and look for "TO LET" signs posted in the windows of many of the row houses there.

On 68th Street, between Central Park West and Columbus Avenue, we found such a sign, and the landlord happened to be outside. He was a friendly, elderly German, and engaged my parents in conversation. He and his wife lived on the ground floor. They were very sympathetic to our plight and eager to rent their furnished room for the enormous price of $20 a week.

They were willing to let us rent because they thought I was a lovely child and could see I was quiet and shy and would give no trouble by being noisy or boisterous. Things were beginning to look good.

The large room was in the back of the building facing a patch of grass in a tiny yard. Its window was covered by a colorless sheer curtain, a threadbare grayish covering on the floor, two beds, three chairs, a table, and a dresser. An adjoining space without a door but a curtain in its place had a toilet, a bathtub, a sink, and a white painted wooden kitchen cabinet, the kind that had little glass panes in its doors above a counter. It was very expensive for our very limited finances but would allow us to be together after many years.

The other factor was the need to get me to school as quickly as possible. The end of the school year was near, and it would have meant being a year behind if I didn't go before it ended. We had to consider distance from a subway station or bus stop, so we could get around the city with ease to get to work and to school. We accepted the terms, not realizing in the excitement of the moment that there was no refrigeration or cooking facility.

In time, eating at the Automat and the necessary mile-long walk each way from 68th street, lost its appeal. It became burdensome in the hot and humid weather of summer, and added to the financial strain of the rent, it was prohibitive. My father had to broach the subject with the landlord to provide refrigeration and a cooking option. At first, he categorically refused to consider the matter. Eventually, he relented, and for additional rent a used refrigerator and a two-burner hotplate was brought in. Now we could prepare our own simple meals and eat in the comfort of our room.

I was enrolled in 7th grade in Joan of Arc Junior High School on 93rd Street and learned to take the city bus. In the evenings, my father helped with my math homework. We sat until midnight, using a dictionary to translate the English text of the word problems to German and make sense of them before I could set up and write the equations.

Now that we were in a country where religion was not taboo, my mother enrolled me in a Talmud Torah at the Spanish and Portuguese Synagogue, only two blocks away on Central Park West. Class was Wednesday afternoons after school. She felt it important to enrich my education by exposing me to awareness of the history of my people and some of the customs that have come down through the millennia.

My father, an architect/engineer, found a job as a shipping clerk with a rag merchant downtown. As worried as my parents were about the future, we cherished being relatively free and began to settle in.

PLAYING WITH ROCKS

Word came of the arrival of 40 new people in our middle-of-nowhere Siberian settlement, and that there were some children. That was good news. I would have someone to play with. There were two girls, Rachel, age 5, same as I, Rivka, 8 years old, and a boy of 6. The newcomers spoke Yiddish; I didn't, but for purposes of play, we managed to make ourselves understood, more or less.

We were on a space where a path led downhill to the river, the same general area where I had lost the mitten in winter. It was gravelly and dusty; sharp pieces of rock that had been pushed aside when the roadbed was cut were lying about. The boy had the idea to play tag by tossing stones at us. Rachel crouched for some reason, and I squatted behind her. When she got up without warning, the rock glanced off her shoulder and hit me in the forehead. I touched the stinging spot gingerly; there was no blood, so I thought nothing of it.

Suddenly, a red torrent spilled over my eyes. In a panic, I began to cry and ran to the cabin to my grandma. She laid me down and brought a cold wet towel to clean me up and soothe me. While I was calming down with the cold compress, she asked questions regarding who threw the rock, and why, and what was my part in causing this to happen? I told her everything, and I also wanted the boy to be punished. Grandma said I had to forgive, that it was not my place to make that decision; it was God's, because He sees and knows everything, including what's in your heart.

I never forgot that, and still find it difficult to believe.

THE AFTERNOON WITH MISS CLAIROL

In the summer of 1952, I had my first job as a counselor in Camp Grottewitt, a children's camp. The pretty, white clapboard house with a porch surrounding its façade overlooking the still pastoral village of Stamford, New York, had once been a family home at the top of a hill in the shadow of Mount Utsayantha. For eight weeks each summer since the 1940s, 3 dozen campers, ages 5 to 12, were supervised and nurtured by a staff of young, devoted counselors presided over by chunky, middle-aged owner/director, Irma Grottewitt; hence, the name of the tiny enterprise.

The kitchen, dining room, and director's quarters were on the ground floor; bedrooms for the girls on the second floor, and the counselors in the attic. Mike, the swimming instructor, the only young male on the premises, was king of all the water activities in and around the pool and slept in a different location. The rec hall, a converted barn, was where we staged theatricals, created crafts projects, and played games on rainy days when the large green outdoor space where the dome of the sky touched the edges of the property was too wet.

I had never been to a camp before. Everything was new to me; the songs, congregate meals, sports, crafts, romantic intrigues, and during the last week, Color War, a traditional fiercely competitive and emotionally draining series of events in which the entire camp population, including the counselors, was divided into two teams, and competed in team and individual sports, art and crafts, and the creating of new lyrics to popular songs. Costumes and presentation were part of the competition. Counselors participated to the fullest, working much more than their hours, staying up very late to help their team be at its best. Everyone was stressed to the limit.

I had gone all my years without ever meeting anyone else named Ruth. Here, there were three of us. That made me very happy, but for purposes of easy identification, we were temporarily renamed Rudy, Ruthie, and Rickie (me).

I had four 10-year old girls under my care. One of them, the daughter of well-known divorced actors, was already an emotional basket-case and a bit of a challenge. The other three were from stable homes in well-to–do Scarsdale and Long Island and were fun and easy to be with.

I met Kitty, a fellow counselor. To my surprise, that was her real name, not a nickname, and there was, indeed, something delicate and kittenish about her. She had spent some years in China and was reared by an Amah, the Chinese equivalent of a nanny. We were both approximately the same height, had just graduated from high school in June, and were brunettes with a hankering to change our hair color to blonde to see if we could have "more fun," as the poster for Clairol hair products promised.

We bought two bottles of Miss Clairol hair lightener when we went to the town drugstore. One sunny afternoon during rest hour, we read the instructions on the package and put our plan into action. We shampooed our hair; towel dried it, poured the stuff on, and combed it through our tresses. We climbed out to the slanted roof outside our attic dorm window and sat in the sun to let its magic help the blonding effort along.

I was a little uneasy about doing this, knowing my mother's absolute taboo regarding any tampering with the natural color of my hair or using make-up. This opportunity was too tempting to resist, especially because I was away from home and had a partner in crime. I figured it would grow out before summer's end.

We sat sweltering on the roof in the midsummer heat until it was time to get back to our campers. Back in the attic, we looked in the mirror. There was no change in my or Kitty's chestnut brown hair. There must have been something we didn't do right.

Part of me was relieved. I didn't have to worry about my mother finding out, and I wouldn't have to be prepared with explanations. But the other part of me was disappointed; thus, I missed that chance to find out how I would look and feel as a blonde.

Later in life, I never gave it another thought. Perhaps I was simply not destined to be a blonde.

GOALS

His lanky, tall body scrunched in the driver's seat, flaxen hair tumbling over his forehead, my self-appointed high school protector cum sweetheart had a triumphant *"look at me and my car!"* expression in his sparkling pale blue eyes and smiling face.

We had not been in touch for a very long time - since I left high school about two years before.

We were the products of a school system that thought it a good idea to start children born in the first part of the year in January, and those born after June in September. Flip was born in February and I in March. That put us on the mid-year graduation track. The approach was being phased out when we were in high school and we were the last class. I went to summer school to get ahead, eager to get to college without waiting a semester. I graduated in June.

Many issues, as well as the fact that I was suddenly "ahead," came between us. Even after three years of five-day-a-week contact in school, we drifted apart. We had not been in touch for nearly two years when he called. By the time he called in the summer of 1954, I was in art school and had just returned from a trip to the six-year-old State of Israel. I was passionate about the pioneer spirit I felt there, bursting with excitement, eager to share my fantastic experience. I agreed to meet with him, expecting to inspire similar feelings.

We rode north on the Westside Highway. In the passenger seat beside him, I searched my brain for appropriate words of praise regarding the car that would please him, but my heart wasn't in it. He seemed to be expecting oohs and aahs of admiration for acquiring the wheels. Frankly, I didn't appreciate the importance of the accomplishment. Living in mid-Manhattan where bus transportation was excellent and parking and maintenance very expensive, a car was a matter of indifference to me at the time.

We parked on a bluff overlooking the Hudson River north of the George Washington Bridge. It was getting dark, that indigo time of the evening. The lights across the river twinkled, a perfect setting for a romantic encounter. He turned the ignition off and looked at me as happy as if he'd been victorious in gladiatorial combat, and now expected the reward of kudos.

For my part, I accepted his invitation chiefly to share the overwhelming enthusiasm that was bubbling over in me for what I had seen and experienced in the young country getting itself organized to function like any other in the world after 2 millennia of the peoples' statelessness.

Clearly, we were bringing different agendas to this encounter. For him, the car must have represented freedom and financial achievement. I failed to catch or understand the significance of the moment for him. I had other "important" things on my mind.

My mission this summer evening was to share the joy and pride I felt about the visit, to have witnessed the hopes in the process of being realized on that arid parcel of land that had been fought over for millennia.

We were at cross purposes, neither of us mature enough to make room for the other. We didn't know how to bridge the gap and share in each other's joy.

"What do you want to do with your life?" I asked bluntly, eager to spill my idealistic beans of confessing a desire to help build the country and perhaps hoping he would want to join me.

His response was unhesitating, "To make a million dollars."

In shock and disappointment, I said flatly, "Take me home."

Suddenly, he looked hard and cruel, his lower jaw moved sideways, and I could see him swallowing. He put the key in the ignition, stepped on the gas, and nothing more was said.

I came home devastated, yet it confirmed my decision back in high school to separate from him. We really had nothing in common.

******

Forty-three years passed before we spoke again. He did indeed make the million many times over, built a successful business, raised a family, and "lived happily ever after." After 17 more years, we established contact as elderly people. Our world view and goals continue to be far apart, but some nostalgia remains. That's another story.

AUTHOR BIO

(photo by Ruth Hohberg, a "selfie")

Born in Krakow, Poland, Ruth L. Weiss Hohberg is a graduate of the Cooper Union School of Art in New York City. She holds a BA from the College of the City of New York; MA from the College of New Rochelle; and MSW from the Wurzweiler School of Social Work of Yeshiva University.

Getting Here: An Odyssey through WWII is a memoir of surviving. In *A Girl from Bielsko*, Ruth continues the story of her life. *Witness and Survivor* is a translation from German of an uncle's memoir. *Going Places* describes some overseas trips. *Vignettes from Life* is a collection short essays on different subjects, as is *Moments and Memories*. She was a member of the American Pen Women, as well as Press Club of North San Diego County until the chapter dissolved.

Ruth's other loves - painting and photography - have won prizes in exhibitions throughout New York, New Jersey, and Connecticut. As an artist, Ruth works in watercolor, acrylic, oil-pastel, pen and ink, colored pencil, and photography. She has also created photo-mosaics and photo-weaves. Her choice of subject matter revolves around nature, architecture, and atmosphere. She moved to San Diego at the end of 2000.

Publication assistance provided by *GSP-Assist*, a service of

Great Spirit Publishing

greatspiritpublishing@yahoo.com